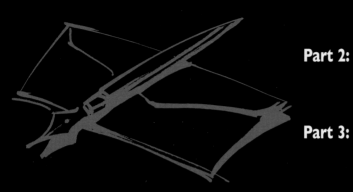

easy

Microsoft® Home Essentials® 98

See it done

Do it yourself

D1409282

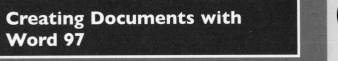

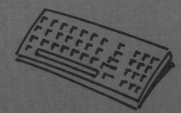

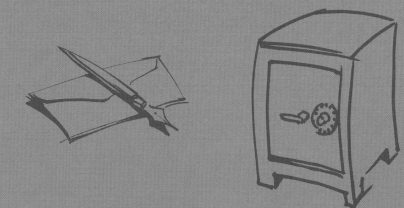

Part ▶ **3: Tracking Your Finances with Money 98**

Easy Microsoft® Home Essentials® 98

Copyright© 1998 by Que® Corporation

All rights reserved. Printed in the United States of America. No part of this book may be used or reproduced in any form or by any means, or stored in a database or retrieval system, without prior written permission of the publisher except in the case of brief quotations embodied in critical articles and reviews. Making copies of any part of this book for any purpose other than your own personal use is a violation of United States copyright laws. For information, address Que Corporation, 201 W. 103rd Street, Indianapolis, IN, 46290. You may reach Que's direct sales line by calling 1-800-428-5331.

Library of Congress Catalog No.: 98-85048

ISBN: 0-7897-1707-7

This book is sold as is, without warranty of any kind, either express or implied, respecting the contents of this book, including but not limited to implied warranties for the book's quality, performance, merchantability, or fitness for any particular purpose. Neither Que Corporation nor its dealers or distributors shall be liable to the purchaser or any other person or entity with respect to any liability, loss, or damage caused or alleged to have been caused directly or indirectly by this book.

99 98   6 5 4 3 2 1

Interpretation of the printing code: the rightmost double-digit number is the year of the book's printing; the rightmost single-digit number, the number of the book's printing. For example, a printing code of 98-1 shows that the first printing of the book occurred in 1998.

All terms mentioned in this book that are known to be trademarks or service marks have been appropriately capitalized. Que cannot attest to the accuracy of this information. Use of a term in this book should not be regarded as affecting the validity of any trademark or service mark.

Screen reproductions in this book were created using Collage Plus from Inner Media, Inc., Hollis, NH.

Excite, Excite Search, and the Excite Logo are trademarks of Excite, Inc. and may be registered in various jurisdictions. Excite screen display copyright 1995-1998 Excite, Inc.

This book was produced digitally by Macmillan Computer Publishing and manufactured using compter-to-plate technology (a film-less process) by GAC/Shepard Poorman, Indianapolis, Indiana.

Executive Editor
Karen Reinisch

Acquisitions Editor
Don Essig

Development Editor
Melanie Palaisa

Technical Editor
Doug Klippert

Managing Editor
Thomas F. Hayes

Project Editor
Lori A. Lyons

Copy Editor
Cliff Shubbs

Indexer
Tim Tate

Book Designer
Jean Bisesi

Cover Designer
Anne Jones

Production Team
Svetlana Dominguez
Trina Wurst

How to Use This Book

It's as Easy as 1-2-3

Each part of this book is made up of a series of short, instructional lessons, designed to help you understand basic information that you need to get the most out of your computer hardware and software.

Click: Click the left mouse button once.

Double-click: Click the left mouse button twice in rapid succession.

Right-click: Click the right mouse button once.

Pointer Arrow: Highlights an item on the screen you need to point to or focus on in the step or task.

Selection: Highlights the area onscreen discussed in the step or task.

Click & Type: Click once where indicated and begin typing to enter your text or data.

 Tips and Warnings give you a heads-up for any extra information you may need while working through the task.

2 Each task includes a series of quick, easy steps designed to guide you through the procedure.

How to Drag: Point to the starting place or object. Hold down the mouse button (right or left per instructions), move the mouse to the new location, then release the button.

1 Each step is fully illustrated to show you how it looks onscreen.

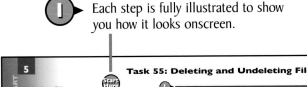

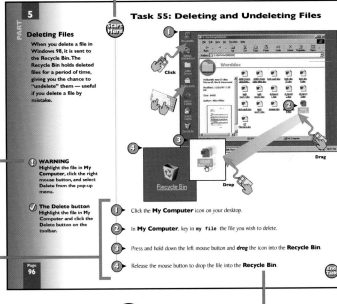

3 Items that you select or click in menus, dialog boxes, tabs, and windows are shown in **Bold**. Information you type is in a **special font**.

 Next Step: If you see this symbol, it means the task you're working on continues on the next page.

 End Task: Task is complete.

Introduction to Microsoft Home Essentials 98

Microsoft Home Essentials 98 offers several different Microsoft programs: Word 97, Works 4.5, Money 98, Internet Explorer 3.02, Greetings Workshop, the Encarta 98 Encyclopedia, and several different games.

This diverse collection of programs helps your computer serve as a resource for every family member who may need it to type a letter, double-check math calculations, or organize names and addresses. You can track your finances, or surf the Internet for entertainment or research. Save shopping time and money by creating personalized cards, stationery, and posters. You can even use the electronic encyclopedia to answer tricky questions or help you work through the crossword puzzle in your local paper.

- Create documents like letters and lists.

- Crunch numbers or keep an address book.

- Track your budget and write checks.

- Visit Web pages.

- Create your own greeting cards and other projects.

- Do research for a report.

- Bone up on Windows.

With your home computer, Microsoft Home Essentials 98, and *Easy Microsoft Home Essentials 98* as your roadmap, you have everything you need to get started. You'll be creating documents and projects like a pro in no time!

PART I

Creating Documents with Word 97

Word processing programs provide tools for creating text-oriented documents such as letters, memos, reports, flyers, newsletters, and so on. The Word 97 skills you and your family members learn can come in handy in a variety of settings—at home, on the job, or at school—wherever you find a computer with Word. This part shows you how to use Word 97 to create a document, improve its appearance, and then print as many hard copies as you need.

Tasks

Task 1: Starting and Exiting Word

Starting and Exiting Word

Windows loads automatically when you start your computer and turn on your monitor, but Word 97 does not. You have to tell your computer and Windows to start Word and display it onscreen. You can then type your document text and use Word's buttons and commands to work with that text. When you finish working with Word, you use another command to exit the Word program so that you can move on to other work.

✓ **Introduce Yourself**
The first time you start Word 97, the User Name dialog box appears. Type your name in the **Name** text box to replace the entry it holds. Press **Tab** and type your initials in the **Initials** text box. Click **OK** to close the dialog box.

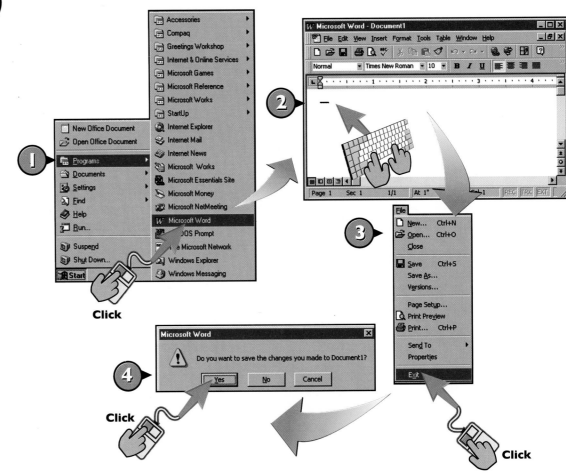

① Click **Start**, point to **Programs**, and then choose **Microsoft Word**.

② When Word 97 opens onscreen, you can type and format your text.

③ Choose **File**, **Exit** or press **Alt+F4** when you're ready to exit Word.

④ If prompted, click **Yes** to save your changes (see Task 21 for more about saving) or **No** to exit.

Task 2: Typing Text in a Document

Start Here

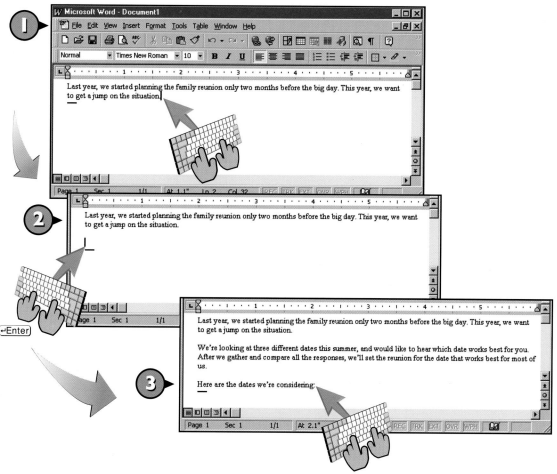

Entering Text

Word 97 makes it easy for you to capture your thoughts. Each keyboard character you press appears at the blinking vertical *insertion point*, which moves to the right as you type. When the text reaches the right margin, the *word wrap* feature automatically moves the insertion point to the next line. Pressing **Enter** starts a new paragraph (called a *paragraph break*), whether that paragraph consists of one line or many lines. When you fill a page, Word 97 automatically inserts a *soft page break* (an automatic page break) to start a new page for you.

ⓘ WARNING

If you're typing and you get an unexpected result, you might have pressed the Ctrl or Alt key instead of the Shift key. Try pressing **Ctrl+Z** to undo the action, or press **Esc** to close any dialog box or menu that appears.

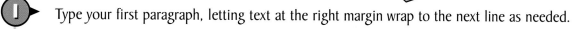

1. Type your first paragraph, letting text at the right margin wrap to the next line as needed.

2. Press **Enter** to start a new paragraph and press **Enter** again, if needed, to insert a blank line.

3. Repeat steps 1 and 2 to type additional paragraphs.

End Task

Page 5

Task 3: Moving the Insertion Point

Moving the Insertion Point

As noted in the last task, whatever you type in Word 97 appears at the location of the flashing vertical insertion point. So it follows that when you want to make changes, you need to move the insertion point to the location of the text to change. After you've moved the insertion point to the correct location, you can use the techniques covered in Task 4, "Making Simple Changes," to edit the text. Moving the insertion point automatically *scrolls* the onscreen text, so you can see what you're editing.

Start Here

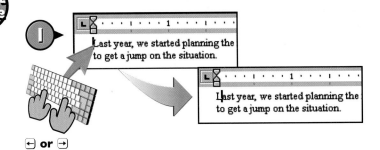

⬅ **or** ➡

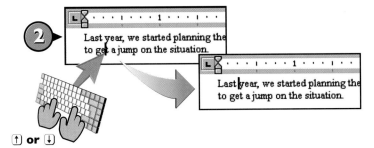

⬆ **or** ⬇

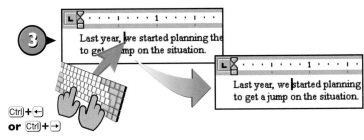

Ctrl+⬅
or Ctrl+➡

✓ Click Your Spot

If you're comfortable using the mouse, you can click with the mouse to position the insertion point in the document.

1 ▶ Press the **left** or **right arrow** key to move the insertion point one character left or right.

2 ▶ Press the **up** or **down arrow** key to move the insertion point one line up or down.

3 ▶ Press **Ctrl+left arrow** or **Ctrl+right arrow** to move the insertion point one word left or right.

Next Step

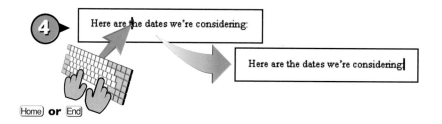

Home or End

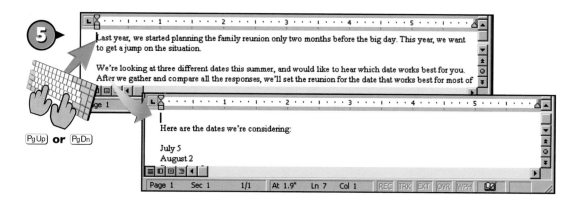

PgUp or PgDn

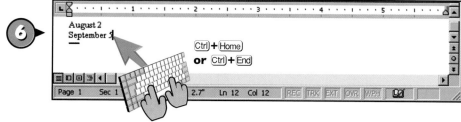

Ctrl + Home
or Ctrl + End

④ Press **Home** or **End** to move the insertion point to the beginning or end of the line holding it.

⑤ Press **PgUp** or **PgDn** to move the insertion point up or down by one screenful of information.

⑥ Press **Ctrl+Home** or **Ctrl+End** to move the insertion point to the beginning or end of the document.

✓ **Using the Scroll Bar**
You can use the vertical scroll bar at the right side of the document to display other areas. Drag the scroll bar box up or down until you see the page number for the page you want to display and then release the mouse button, or click the up or down arrow on the bar to scroll in either direction. You also can click the **Previous Page** or **Next Page** buttons (each has a double-arrow) at the bottom of the scroll bar to display the previous or next page.

① **WARNING**
Keep in mind that scrolling the document does not move the insertion point. After you use the vertical scroll bar or the Previous Page or Next Page buttons to scroll the document, click to position the insertion point in the onscreen text.

Making Changes to Text

Even though word processors like Word 97 offer a host of fancy features, you can do most of your editing work using a few simple techniques. You can use the keyboard to make many changes to your text, either as you're typing or at a later time when you're working with the document. For most users, the keyboard remains the primary editing tool because you can make your changes without lifting a hand to work with the mouse.

(✓) **Working with a Text Block**

You can select a block of text and then delete, replace, move, or copy the whole thing. Tasks 5 through 8 cover these techniques.

Task 4: Making Simple Changes

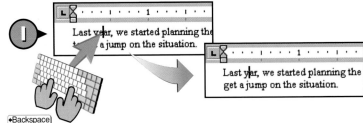

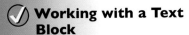

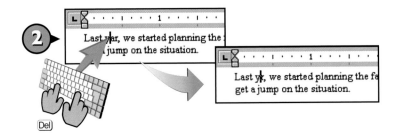

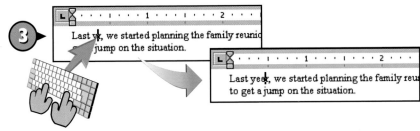

1 ▶ Click to position the insertion point after the letter you want to remove. Press the **Backspace** key to remove the character to the left of the insertion point.

2 ▶ Press the **Delete** key to remove the character to the right of the insertion point.

3 ▶ Type new text to add it at the insertion point.

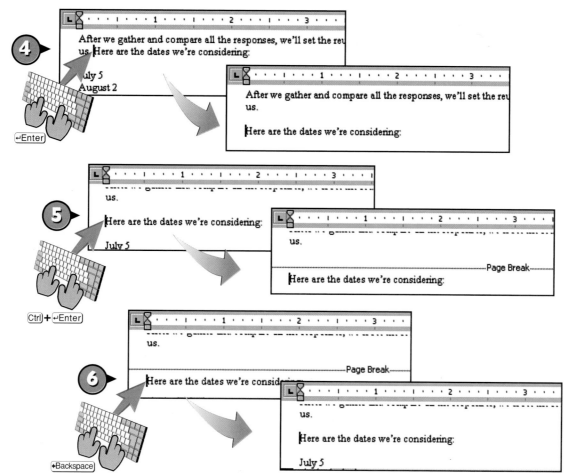

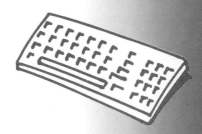

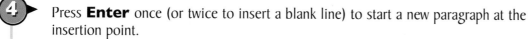 **Controlling Page Breaks**

If you add or remove a large amount of text in a document, Word 97 automatically inserts and removes soft (automatic) page breaks. You can force or insert a *hard page break* (also called a *manual page break*) where you need it, as described in step 5.

4 Press **Enter** once (or twice to insert a blank line) to start a new paragraph at the insertion point.

5 Click to position the insertion point where you want to start a new page, and then press **Ctrl+Enter**.

6 Click after a page or paragraph break or blank line, and then press **Backspace** to delete it.

Tabbing Over

Press **Tab** to move the insertion point to the next tab stop (preset alignment measurement), so that you can type text starting at the tab stop. By default, Word 97 has a tab stop set every 0.5".

Task 5: Selecting Text

Selecting Text

Rather than working a word or character at a time, you can *select* a larger amount of text so that actions you perform—including editing and formatting actions—are applied to the entire selection. Word 97 offers a number of different mouse and keyboard techniques for selecting text. Because black reverse highlighting appears over the selected text, you may also hear folks use the words *highlighting* text to describe making a selection.

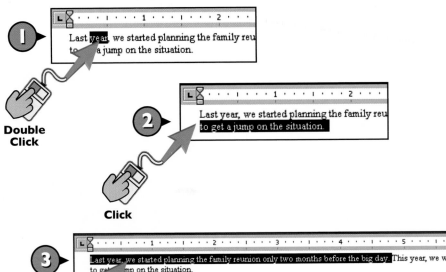

Double Click

Click

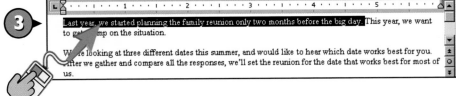

Ctrl +Click

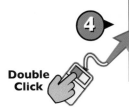

Double Click

(!) WARNING

Be careful when you select text. If you accidentally press a key while you have a selection highlighted, you could obliterate the whole selection. Immediately press **Ctrl+Z** to get it back.

① Double-click any word to select it.

② Click in the left margin next to a line to select the line.

③ Press and hold **Ctrl** and click a sentence to select the whole sentence.

④ Double-click in the left margin next to a paragraph to select the whole paragraph.

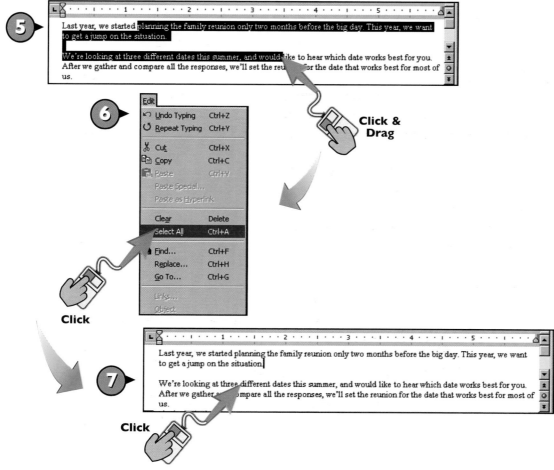

(5)

Last year, we started planning the family reunion only two months before the big day. This year, we want to get a jump on the situation.

We're looking at three different dates this summer, and would like to hear which date works best for you. After we gather and compare all the responses, we'll set the reunion for the date that works best for most of us.

Click & Drag

(6)

Edit

↶ Undo Typing	Ctrl+Z
↻ Repeat Typing	Ctrl+Y
✄ Cut	Ctrl+X
📋 Copy	Ctrl+C
📋 Paste	Ctrl+V
Paste Special...	
Paste as Hyperlink	
Clear	Delete
Select All	Ctrl+A
🔍 Find...	Ctrl+F
Replace...	Ctrl+H
Go To...	Ctrl+G
Links...	
Object	

Click

(7)

Last year, we started planning the family reunion only two months before the big day. This year, we want to get a jump on the situation.

We're looking at three different dates this summer, and would like to hear which date works best for you. After we gather and compare all the responses, we'll set the reunion for the date that works best for most of us.

Click

(5) Drag over an irregular block of text to select it.

(6) Choose **Edit**, **Select All** to select all the document text.

(7) To cancel a selection, click outside the selection in another area of the document.

✓ **Selecting an Irregular Area**
To choose an irregular selection, you also can click at the beginning of the block, scroll to display the end of the block to select, press and hold **Shift**, and then click at the end of the block. This technique works better if you find that your screen scrolls too quickly when you try to make a selection by dragging alone.

✓ **Selecting with the Keyboard**
To use the keyboard alone to make a selection, press and hold **Shift**, then press any arrow key to extend the selection. Or, press and hold **Shift+Ctrl**, then press the **up** or **down arrow** keys to extend the selection by a paragraph at a time.

End Task

Task 6: Deleting and Replacing Text

Deleting and Replacing Text

Word 97 offers a few different techniques you can use to correct text in a document more quickly. For starters, you can delete a whole selection—even all the text in the document if you've selected all of it. By default, Word works in **Insert mode**, meaning that text you type appears at the insertion point, and existing text moves further right. To replace the text to the right instead of moving it, you can turn on **Overtype mode** and type the replacement information.

✓ **But It Was a Mistake!**
If you make a mistake while deleting or replacing text, you can undo it. See Task 9, "Undoing and Redoing a Change," to learn how to fix mistakes.

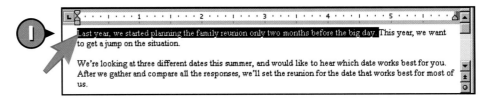

Last year, we started planning the family reunion only two months before the big day. This year, we want to get a jump on the situation.

We're looking at three different dates this summer, and would like to hear which date works best for you. After we gather and compare all the responses, we'll set the reunion for the date that works best for most of us.

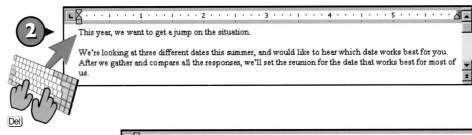

This year, we want to get a jump on the situation.

We're looking at three different dates this summer, and would like to hear which date works best for you. After we gather and compare all the responses, we'll set the reunion for the date that works best for most of us.

Del

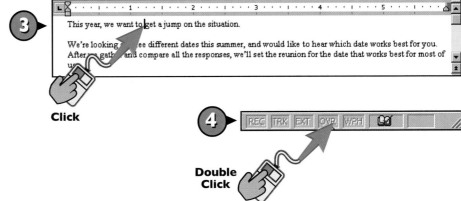

This year, we want to get a jump on the situation.

We're looking at three different dates this summer, and would like to hear which date works best for you. After we gather and compare all the responses, we'll set the reunion for the date that works best for most of us.

Click

| REC | TRK | EXT | OVR | WPH | 📖 | |

Double Click

1. Select the text to delete.

2. Press **Delete** to delete selected text.

3. Click to place the insertion point just before the text to replace.

4. Double-click the **OVR** indicator on the status bar or press **Insert** to turn on Overtype mode.

Next Step

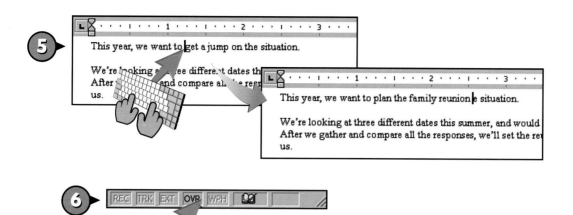

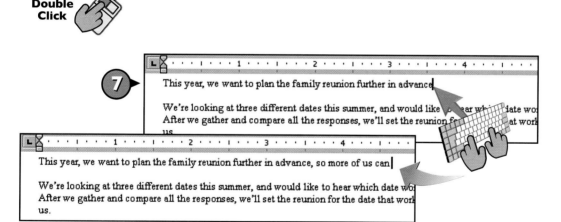

5. Type to replace text to the right of the insertion point in overtype mode.

6. Double-click the **OVR** indicator on the status bar or press **Insert** to return to Insert mode.

7. Type to insert new text at the insertion point location.

WARNING
If you have some text selected when typing in either Insert mode or Overtype mode, your first keypress replaces the entire selection. If you don't want to replace the selection, click to move the insertion point before you type.

WARNING
When you're working in Overtype mode, be sure to watch how much you type. As long as Overtype mode is active, your typing replaces text to the right of the insertion point. You don't want to type over information that you need to keep, which is easy to do in Overtype mode.

End Task

Task 7: Moving Text

Cutting and Pasting Text

When you move information in Word 97 (and other Windows applications), you remove it from its current location and insert it into its new location. *Cutting* **a selection removes it from the document and places it in the Windows** *Clipboard***. The Clipboard serves as a holding area for cut information until you** *paste* **the information at its new location. You can cut and paste information more quickly than you can delete and retype it. The tools for cutting and pasting text appear on the Standard toolbar, the top toolbar that appears in Word 97.**

⚠ WARNING

After you move text, double-check the area from which you cut the text and the area to which you pasted it to see whether you need to insert or delete any extra spaces.

Start Here

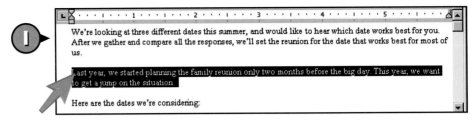

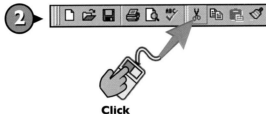

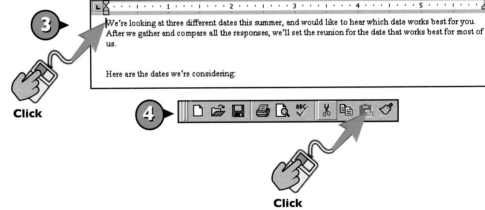

1 ▶ Select the text to move.

2 ▶ Click the **Cut** button to remove the selection from the document and place it on the Clipboard.

3 ▶ Click to place the insertion point where you want to insert the cut text.

4 ▶ Click the **Paste** button to paste the text at its new location.

Task 8: Copying Text

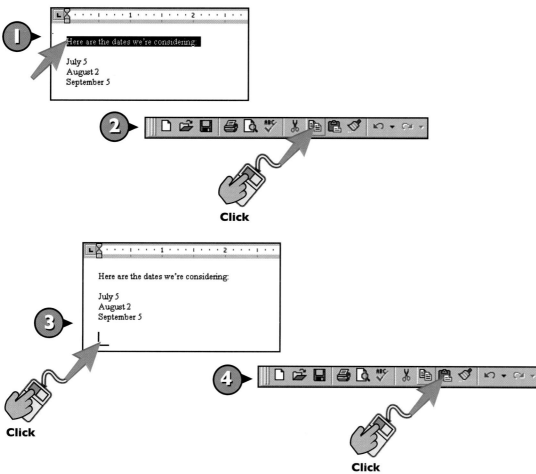

Click

Click

Click

Copying Text

You can copy information at its present location and insert the copy into a new location. Copying a selection duplicates it and places the copy in the Windows *Clipboard*. It remains in the Clipboard holding area until you *paste* the copied information at its new location. You can copy information much more quickly than you can type it.

1 Select the text to copy.

2 Click the **Copy** button to remove the selection from the document and place it on the Clipboard.

3 Click to place the insertion point where you want to insert the copy of the text.

4 Click the **Paste** button to paste the text at its new location.

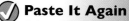

Paste It Again
After you cut or copy information to the Clipboard, you can paste it into multiple locations. The information remains on the Clipboard until you cut or copy something new; the new information replaces the older Clipboard contents.

Task 9: Undoing and Redoing a Change

Using Undo and Redo

If you make a mistake while working with text, use the *Undo* feature to cancel the change and reinstate the text to its prior state. You can undo either the change you just made or several recent changes. Word 97 keeps a list of your changes. When you choose a change to undo from this list, Word 97 undoes that change, plus all changes above it in the list. If you undo a change but decide to reinstate it, you can use *Redo*. If you undid several actions, they appear in a list, and you can redo one or more of them.

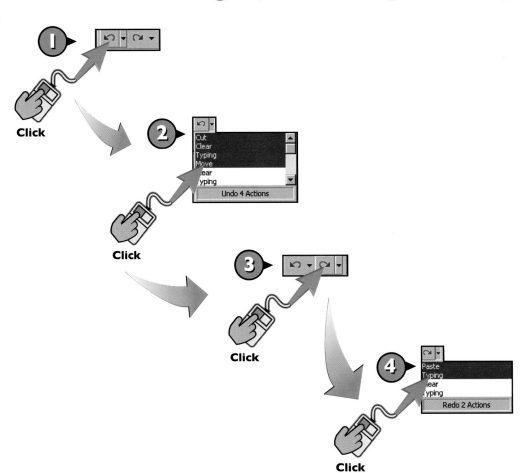

Start Here

Click

Click

Click

Click

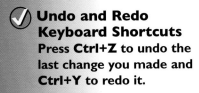 **Undo and Redo Keyboard Shortcuts**
Press **Ctrl+Z** to undo the last change you made and **Ctrl+Y** to redo it.

 Click the **Undo** button to undo your most recent change.

 Click the **Undo drop-down arrow**, then click an action or change to undo it and the changes above it.

 Click the **Redo** button to redo your most recent change.

 Click the **Redo drop-down arrow**, and then click a change to redo it and the changes above it.

 End Task

Task 10: Making a Change with Drag and Drop

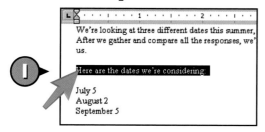

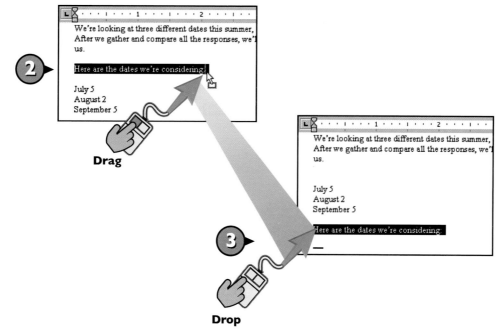

Drag

Drop

Using Drag and Drop

If you need to move text a short distance, you can simply drag it from one location to another with *drag-and-drop* editing. After you become comfortable with the mouse, it's likely you'll use a combination of keyboard techniques, toolbar buttons, and drag and drop to make changes in your document.

⚠ **WARNING**
It's a little tough to control document scrolling while you drag and drop. So use drag and drop to make a change within a sentence or paragraph, and use cut and paste for moves between different pages.

✓ **Drag and Drop a Copy**
You can copy a selection with drag and drop. Press and hold the **Ctrl** key before you press the left mouse button. Hold down the **Ctrl** key while you drag. When you release the mouse button to drop the text, Word inserts a copy of the original selection.

1 Select the text to move.

2 Press and hold the left mouse button and drag the text. A box appears beside the mouse pointer as you drag. Drag until the gray insertion point appears where you want to insert the text.

3 Release the mouse button to drop the text into place.

Adding or Removing Text Formatting

When you change the appearance of a word, paragraph, or page, you're changing its *formatting*. Many beginners start out making modest format changes—say, applying **boldface**, *italic*, or underlining to a few words for emphasis. You may see boldface, italic, and underlining called "attributes."

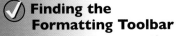 **Finding the Formatting Toolbar**
Use the buttons on the Formatting toolbar to apply formatting changes to text. The Formatting toolbar appears below the Standard (top) toolbar. The Bold, Italic, and Underline buttons described in this task appear on the Formatting toolbar.

Task 11: Adding or Removing Boldface, Italic, or Underlining

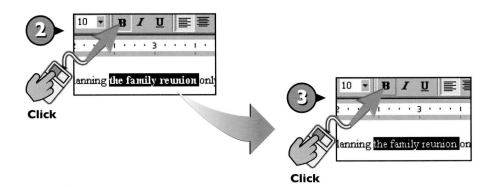

Click

Click

1 ▸ Select the text to format.

2 ▸ Click the **Bold** button.

3 ▸ Click the **Bold** button again to remove the boldface.

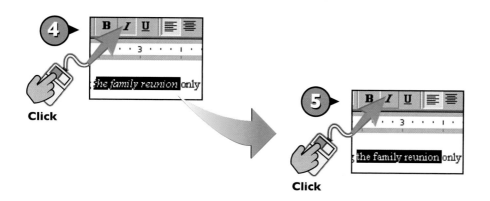

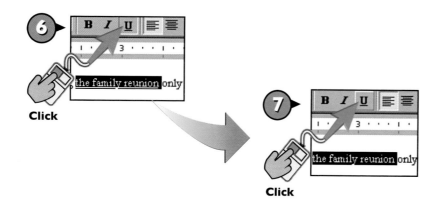

Formatting Keyboard Shortcuts
You can press **Ctrl+B** to apply or remove boldface, **Ctrl+I** to apply italic, and **Ctrl+U** to apply underlining.

Applying Attributes as You Type
You can turn boldface, italic, or underlining on to apply them to text as you type. **Click the toolbar button(s) for the attribute(s) to turn on, type the text, and click the button(s) again to turn the attribute off.**

Clearing Attributes
If you want to remove multiple attributes from a selection simultaneously, press **Ctrl+Spacebar**.

4 ▶ Click the **Italic** button.

5 ▶ Click the **Italic** button again to remove the italic.

6 ▶ Click the **Underline** button.

7 ▶ Click the **Underline** button again to remove the underlining.

Changing Font

The *font* determines the distinctive shape and weight of characters. You can apply any font that's installed in Windows to a selection in a Word document.

✅ Using the Font Dialog Box

If you want to change numerous different formatting selections at once—such as the font, attributes, and more—choose **Format, Font**. Change the settings you want on the Font tab in the Font dialog box. The Preview area shows how the current settings look. Click **OK** to finish changing the settings.

⚠ WARNING

Using too many fonts in a single document makes it look like a ransom note. Generally, stick with one font for headings (titles), another for body text, and perhaps a third to accent selected areas.

Task 12: Choosing Another Font (Look) for Text

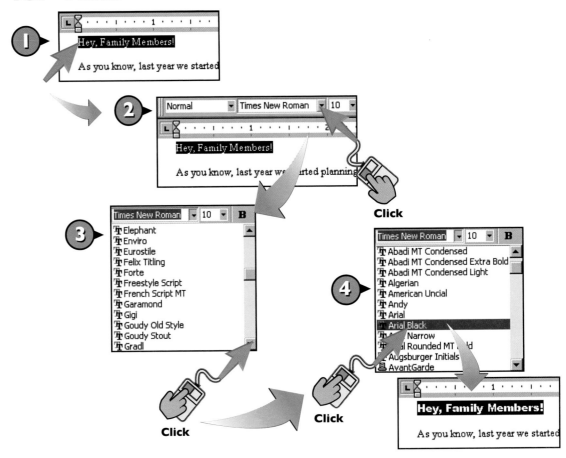

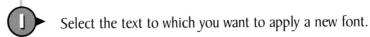

Select the text to which you want to apply a new font.

Click the **Font drop-down list arrow** on the Formatting toolbar.

Use the scroll arrows on the list to display the font you want.

Click the font you want to apply to the selection.

Task 13: Choosing Another Size for Text

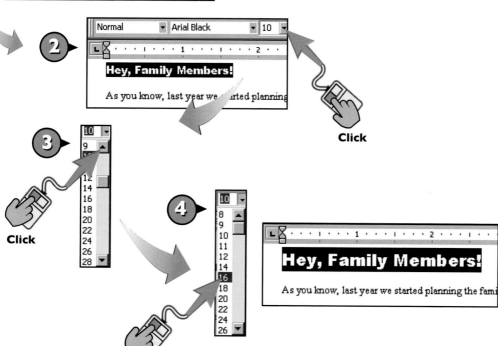

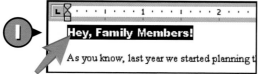

Click

Changing Text Size

You can make text larger to make it more readable or smaller to fit more on a page. Windows applications measure text size in points, with each point equal to 1/72 of an inch.

Click

Click

1. Select the text to which you want to apply a new font size.

2. Click the **Font Size drop-down list arrow** on the Formatting toolbar.

3. Use the scroll arrows on the list to display the size you want.

4. Click the font you want to apply it to the selection.

 Entering a Font Size
Rather than opening and scrolling the Font Size list, you can click in the Font Size text box on the Formatting toolbar, type the size you want (in points), and press Enter.

Task 14: Choosing How Text Lines Up

Aligning Text

Every printed page has blank space around the edges called the margin. You can control how each paragraph of text aligns relative to the left and right margins. **Align Left** lines up each line in a paragraph along the left margin, and is the default setting. **Center** positions each line of text in the paragraph equidistant between the margins. **Align Right** pushes each line of text in the paragraph against the right margin. **Justify** adds spacing within each line so that both sides of the paragraph line up to the margin. By default, text aligns to the left margin, but you can change the alignment.

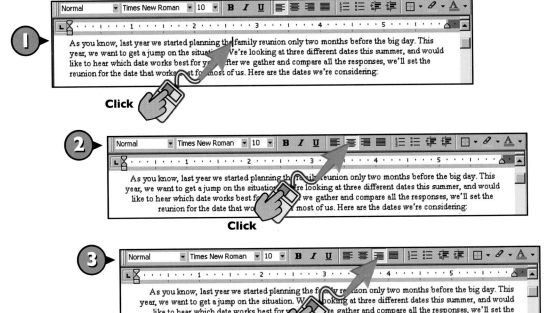

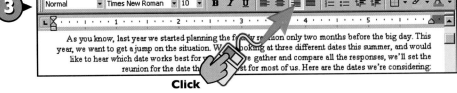

1 ▶ Click in the paragraph to align or select multiple paragraphs to align.

2 ▶ Click the **Center** button on the Formatting toolbar to center the text.

3 ▶ Click the **Align Right** button on the Formatting toolbar to right-align the text.

4 ▶ Click the **Justify** button on the Formatting toolbar to justify the text. Click the **Align Left** button to return to the default setting.

Task 15: Applying a Color to Text

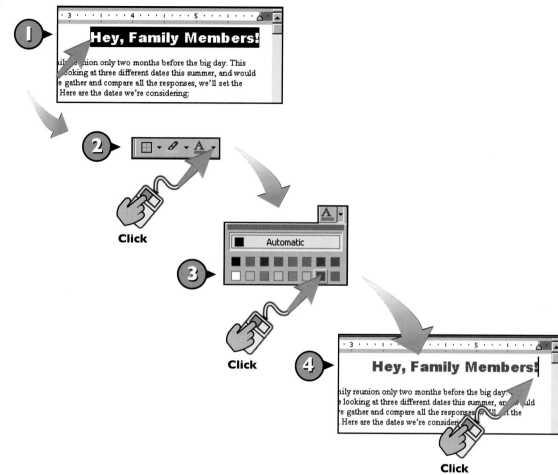

Click

Click

Click

Adding Color to Text

You can change the color of a text selection to help that text stand out from surrounding text. As with the other formatting choices described so far, use a limited number of colors to ensure that the document remains readable and attractive. You'll achieve the best results if you apply color only to headings or titles, and words you want to emphasize.

ⓘ WARNING

Obviously, light colors are hard to read onscreen or on white paper, so if you're emailing a file, providing it to another user on-disk, or printing it, you should go with bold colors that are easy to read. Otherwise, let your printer's capabilities dictate your color choices. Black and white printers convert colors to shades of gray, but some older printers don't handle the process well.

1 ▶ Select the text to which you want to apply a new color.

2 ▶ Click the **Font Color drop-down list arrow** at the far right end of the Formatting toolbar.

3 ▶ Click the color you want in the palette to select it and apply it to the selection.

4 ▶ Click outside the selection to see the color.

End Task

PART
1

Task 16: Changing Spacing Between Lines

Changing Line Spacing

By default, Word uses single-line spacing in the paragraphs you type. That is, each line is about the same height as the font size, with a bit of spacing thrown in to accommodate capital letters and make text readable. You can select one or more paragraphs in the document and change the line spacing, increasing the spacing to 1.5 lines or double-spacing.

✓ **Fine-Tuning Paragraph Spacing**
Rather than pressing **Enter**, you can insert a precise amount of extra space before or after a paragraph. To do so, enter the desired amount of spacing, in points, in the **Before** or **After** text box of the Indents and Spacing tab in the Paragraph dialog box.

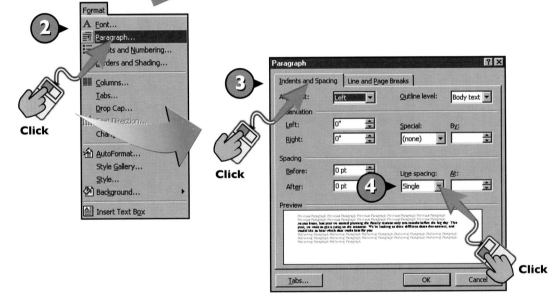

Click

Click

Click

1 Select the paragraph(s) for which you want to change the spacing.

2 Choose **Format**, **Paragraph**.

3 Click the **Indents and Spacing** tab.

4 Click the **Line Spacing drop-down list arrow**.

Page
24

Next Step

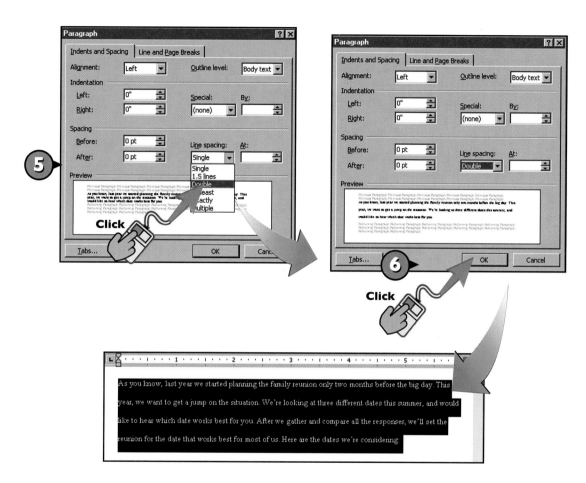

5 Click the spacing choice you want.

6 Click **OK** to close the dialog box and apply the spacing.

WARNING
If you press **Enter** an extra time between paragraphs to insert a blank line and then apply double spacing, keep in mind that you'll end up with four lines' worth of space between paragraphs.

Using Bullets and Numbers

You can create attractive numbered or bulleted lists with a single mouse click. Applying numbers or bullets not only inserts the number or bullet, but also properly indents each item in the list for a neat appearance. Word numbers or bullets each paragraph in the selection to which you add bullets or numbers. To insert additional items within the list, press **Enter**. Word creates the new list item (paragraph).

Task 17: Adding and Removing Bullets and Numbers

Start Here

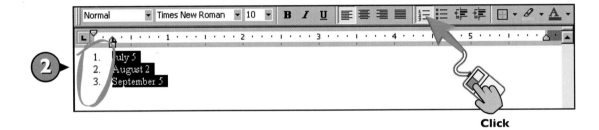

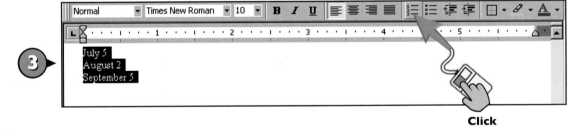

Select the paragraph(s) to which you want to apply numbers or bullets.

Click the **Numbering** button on the Formatting toolbar to apply numbering.

Click the **Numbering** button to remove numbering from a selection.

Next Step

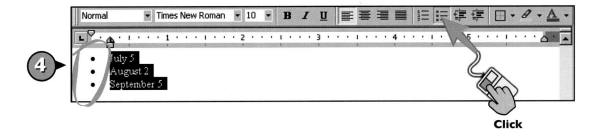

Click

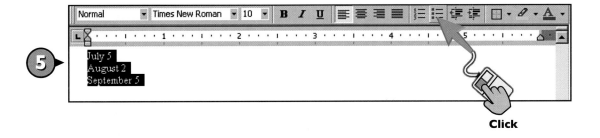

Click

Turning Off Bullets or Numbers
If you press **Enter** at the end of a bulleted or numbered paragraph to create a new paragraph, Word assigns a bullet or number to the new paragraph, too. To stop the bulleting or numbering, click the Numbering or Bullets button to turn off that feature.

④ ► Click the **Bullets** button on the Formatting toolbar to apply bullets.

⑤ ► Click the **Bullets** button to remove bullets from a selection.

Task 18: Inserting a Clip Art Picture

Inserting Clip Art

Word 97 includes a number of predrawn pictures, called *clip art*, that you can insert into a document. Even if you're not an artistic genius or don't have access to images from another source, you can add attractive, colorful images to any document. The Word Clip Gallery divides the clip art into categories, such as Animals, Entertainment, and Household. First choose the category to see the pictures it holds and choose the picture to insert into the document.

Start Here

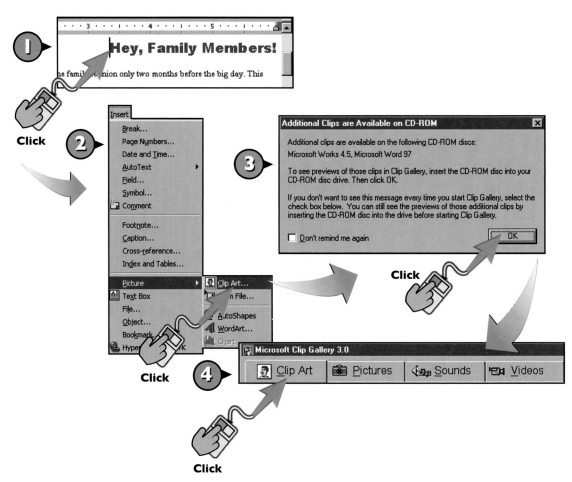

Click

✓ **Stop the Setup Program**
If the Microsoft Home Essentials setup program starts when you insert the CD-ROM, click the Exit Setup button. You don't have to insert the CD-ROM to have clip art available, but Word offers more images if you do.

1 ▶ Click to position the insertion point at the approximate location where you want to place the clip art.

2 ▶ Choose **Insert**, **Picture**, **Clip Art**.

3 ▶ If you want to view more clip art images, insert the Word CD-ROM (Disc I) as directed and click **OK**.

4 ▶ Click the **Clip Art** tab.

Next Step

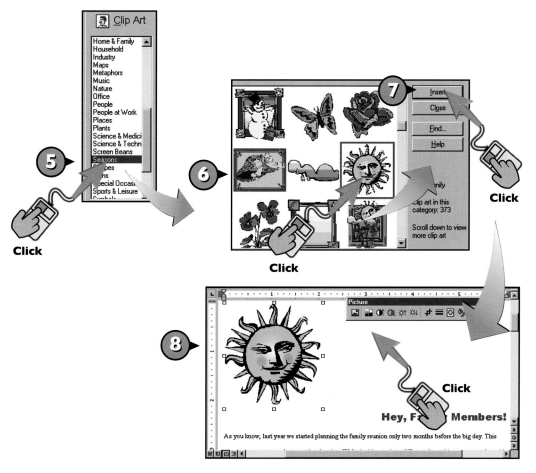

5 ▶ Scroll the list of categories and click a category to see the images it offers.

6 ▶ Scroll the image preview area and click the clip art image you want to insert.

7 ▶ Click the **Insert** button.

8 ▶ Click outside the clip art image to deselect it and hide the picture toolbar.

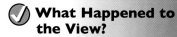

✅ What Happened to the View?
When you insert a clip art picture, Word changes to the Page Layout view. Task 27 covers how to move between the Page Layout and Normal views.

Task 19: Creating WordArt

Creating WordArt

If you want to call attention to a phrase or headline in a document—I mean really make it stand out—mere color and font changes won't do the job. Instead, you can create *WordArt*, which enables you to choose a special effect look for text you enter. WordArt text can be curved, 3D, shadowed, or all three.

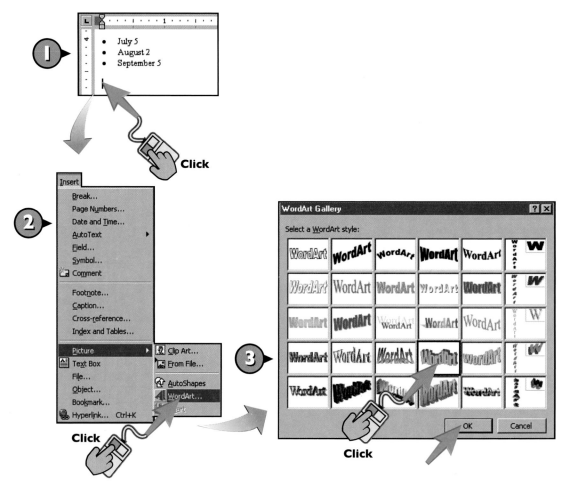

⚠ WARNING

Use clip art and WordArt sparingly. Although no one wants to rain on your creativity, too much artwork may not only distract your reader, but also make your files very large. In fact, you could make a file so large that it wouldn't fit on a floppy disk—a problem if you need to take the file to work or copy it to another computer.

1 Click to position the insertion point at the approximate location where you want to create the WordArt.

2 Choose **Insert**, **Picture**, **WordArt**.

3 In the WordArt Gallery dialog box, click the WordArt look you want, and then click **OK**.

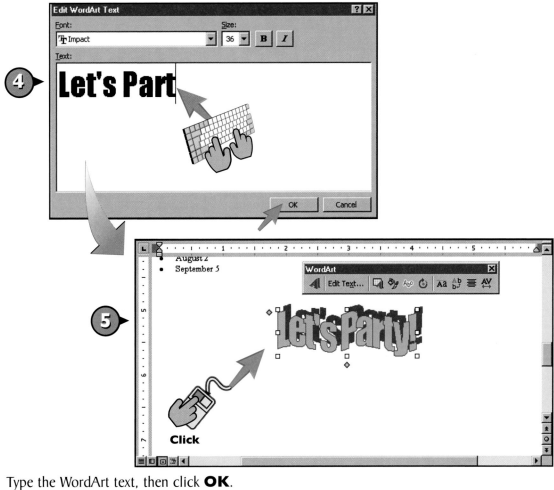

4 ▸ Type the WordArt text, then click **OK**.

5 ▸ Click outside the WordArt image to deselect it and hide the picture toolbar.

✔️ **Formatting WordArt Text**
Before you type your WordArt text, you can use the Font and Size drop-down lists and the Bold and Italic buttons to adjust the look of the text.

✔️ **Keep Your WordArt Simple**
WordArt works best for short, snappy statements. If you try to cram too much into a WordArt object, it may not be readable. Plus, WordArt objects can be large and leave little room for regular text in your document.

Checking Spelling and Grammar

With typewriters, spelling and grammar errors were difficult to correct. In a Word processor, you can easily make changes before you print. You don't even have to proofread your own documents or get a style book to check your sentence structure. Word can check your spelling and grammar for you.

ⓘ WARNING

The spelling and grammar check capabilities in Word can save you a lot of time and embarrassment. However, you should not rely on them alone to make your documents accurate. Checking spelling and grammar doesn't catch certain types of mistakes, such as if you tell someone to "turn North" instead of "turn South" in a memo giving directions to a meeting location or if you confuse similar words like "there" and "their." Always proofread your documents for accuracy.

Task 20: Checking Your Spelling and Grammar

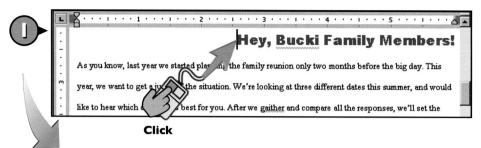

Click

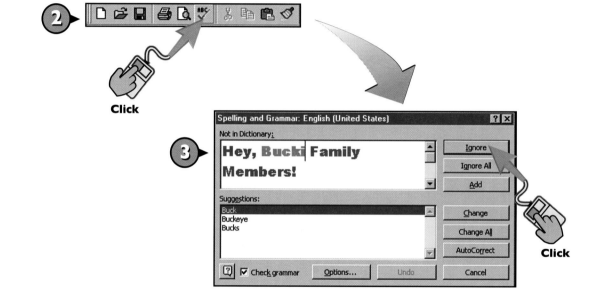

Click

Click

 Click to position the insertion point at the beginning of the text to check.

 Click the **Spelling and Grammar** button on the Standard toolbar.

 If the word(s) highlighted in the Not in Dictionary list does not need correction, click **Ignore**.

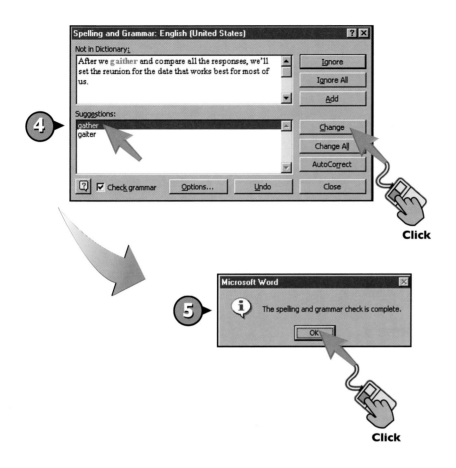

Click

Click

 End Task

4 If the word(s) highlighted in the Not in Dictionary list needs to be changed, click the correct suggestion in the Suggestions list, and then click **Change**.

5 After you repeat steps 4 and 5 to correct all the spelling and grammar mistakes, click **OK** to conclude the check.

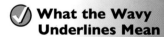 **What the Wavy Underlines Mean**
If you see a wavy red underline below a word, it means that Word thinks it may be misspelled. A wavy green underline under a phrase means that there may be a grammar error in the underlined text. Right-click the underlined word, and click the correct spelling or grammar change in the shortcut menu that appears. Word then corrects the word.

Saving and Naming a File

You need to save your document file to give it a name and store the file on a hard or floppy disk. You can save your Word files in the default disk and folder c:\My Documents\, or another disk or folder of your choosing. Your filenames can be very descriptive because they can include more than 200 characters, spaces, and special capitalization.

 A Gentle Reminder to Save

If you forget to save your changes and try to exit Word, Word reminds you to save the file.

 Up to a Higher Folder

If you're viewing the contents of a folder within a disk and want to back up to see the list of all the folders in the disk, click the **Up One Level** button on the dialog box's toolbar. This is called "moving up a level in the folder tree."

Task 21: Saving and Naming Your Document File

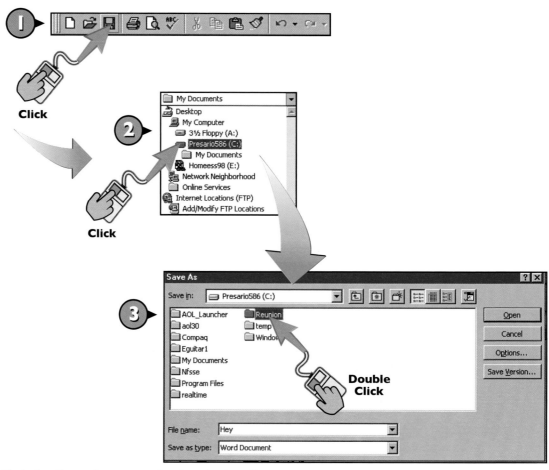

Click

Click

Double Click

Click the **Save** button on the Standard toolbar.

To save to a disk or folder other than the default one, click it in the **Save In** list.

If the disk or folder you selected contains other folders, double-click the one to save to in the list.

Next Step

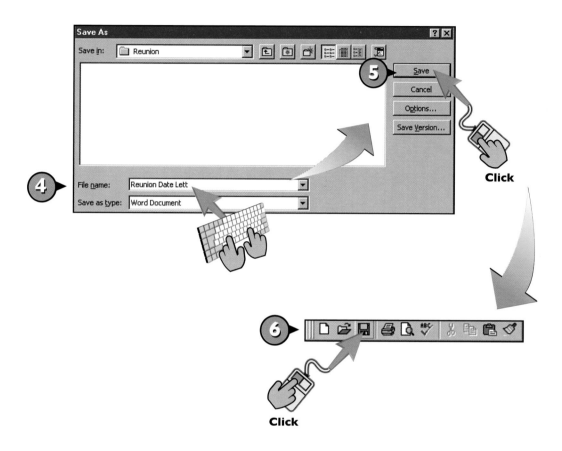

Click

Click

✅ Save as You Go
After you save your file the first time, you should save it every 10 minutes or so thereafter. This helps ensure that you won't lose as much work if your system reboots due to power fluctuations or crashes.

✅ Copying a File
After you save a file the first time, you can choose **File, Save As** to redisplay the Save As dialog box. If you enter a new **File Name** and then click **Save**, Word saves a copy of the file under the new name. Note that any folder you selected previously appears in the Save In text box in the redisplayed Save As dialog box. To save to another folder, use the Save In list to select it. After you save and name the file, its name appears in the Word title bar.

④ ▶ Drag over and then edit the suggested filename in the **File Name text box**.

⑤ ▶ Click the **Save** button.

⑥ ▶ To resave the file after you've saved it the first time, click the **Save** button on the Standard toolbar.

Task 22: Closing a Document File

Closing a File

When you finish working with a file, you should close it to remove it from your computer's memory. Closing also prevents you from making unwanted changes to the document.

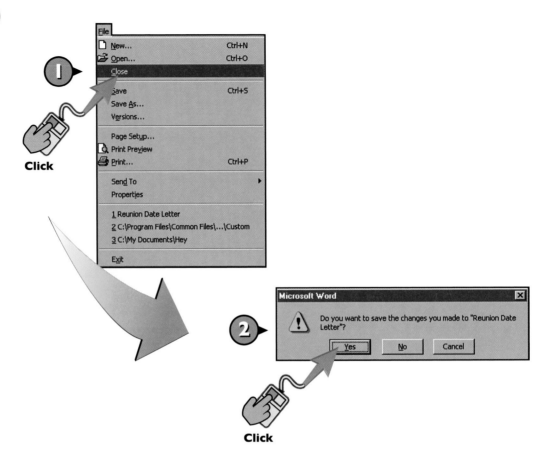

Click

Click

 Choose **File**, **Close**.

 If the file contains changes you haven't saved, click **Yes** to save your changes.

Task 23: Creating a New, Blank Document

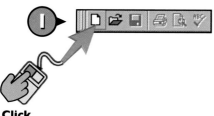

Start Here

Click

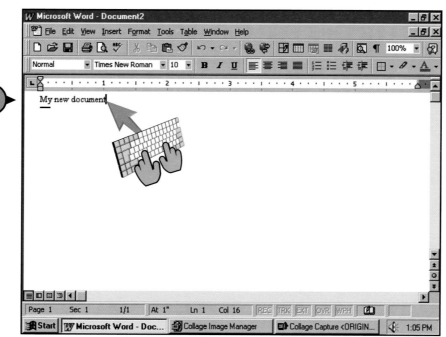

Creating a New Document

To create a new document, you begin by opening a new document file. Word offers different ways to do this. The simplest method creates a blank file that uses default settings for margins, text font and size, and other features. Word assigns a temporary name to each new document you create—Document1, Document2, and so on. (When you start Word, it automatically opens a new, blank Document1 document.) You must save the document to give it a unique name.

① Click the **New** button on the Standard toolbar.

② Start entering content in the new document.

✓ Other New Document Methods

Tasks 24 and 25 present alternative ways for creating new documents.

! WARNING

Don't choose **File, New** to create a blank document. This method requires extra steps.

End Task

Page **37**

Opening an Existing Document

After you create, save, and close a file, you don't have access to it. If you want to make changes to the file or print it, you need to open it in Word. You tell Word which file to open and where it's stored, and then Word redisplays it. After you make any changes, don't forget to click the **Save** button to save those changes.

✓ A File's Path

The disk, folder, and filename combined form the path to the file. For example, if you've saved a file named **Study Guide** in the **School** folder on your hard disk drive (**C:**), that file's path is **C:\School\ Study Guide**. Note that you use backslash characters to separate the parts of the path.

Task 24: Opening a Document You Created Earlier

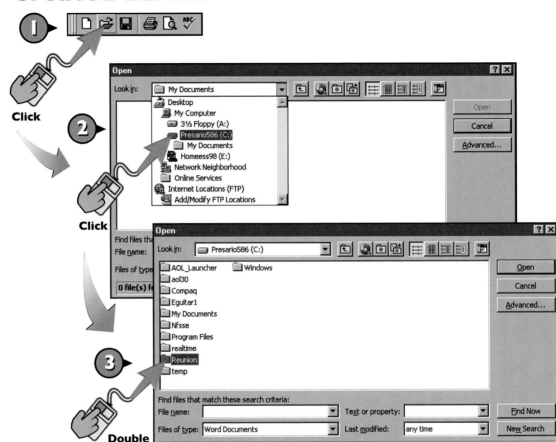

Start Here

Click

Click

Double Click

1. Click the **Open** button on the Standard toolbar.

2. If you previously saved the file to a disk or folder other than the one that appears, click it in the **Look In** list.

3. If the disk or folder you selected contains other folders, double-click the one that holds the file to open in the list.

Next Step

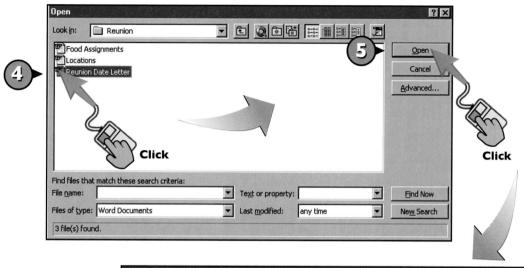

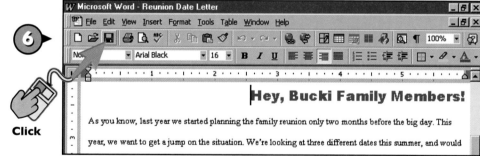

Click

Click

Click

4 Click the icon beside the file to select the file.

5 Click the **Open** button.

6 To resave the file after you've worked with it, click the **Save** button on the Standard toolbar.

WARNING

If you're opening a file that's on a floppy disk (or other type of removable disk), make sure you insert the disk in the drive before you start the process for opening a file. Otherwise, you'll see a message that Word can't find the disk. It's also preferable to save a copy of the file to your hard disk and work on the copy stored on the hard disk. The hard disk provides Word with more "working space" for the file, possibly preventing file corruption. Plus, it's never a good policy to store files only on floppy disk; because your hard disk is safely within your system, it tends to be a safer storage area.

Creating a Document from a Template

You can use Word 97 *templates* to create particular types of documents. Templates generally include attractive formatting. Some include starter text or prompt you to enter text in particular locations. Others also include graphical elements. Word organizes templates in categories.

ⓘ WARNING
You can't use the New button on the Standard toolbar to create a document file based on a template. That button creates a blank document file.

✓ Where to Learn About Wizards
If the template you think you want includes "Wizard" in its name, it's actually an automated template called a *wizard*. Learn more about document wizards in Task 26.

Task 25: Creating a Document from a Template

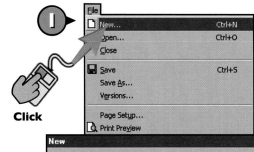

Start Here

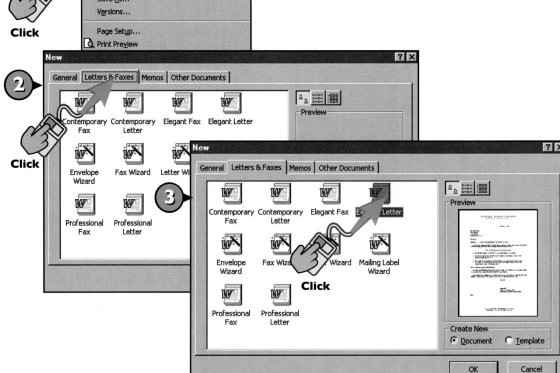

Choose **File**, **New** (Ctrl+N).

Click the tab for the template category you want in order to see the templates in that category.

Click the icon for the template you want to see a preview of.

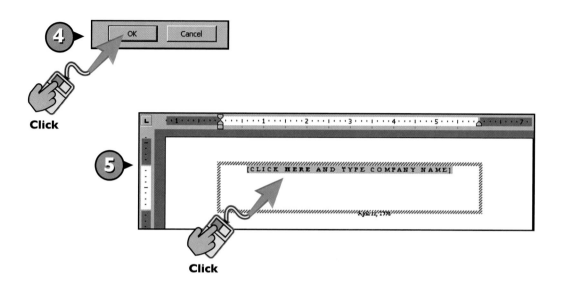

Click

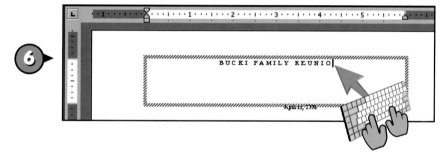

Click

4 ▶ Click **OK** to open a new document based on the template.

5 ▶ Click a prompt.

6 ▶ Type to fill in the prompt, and then click outside of it to finish using it.

⚠ **WARNING**
After you create a document from a template, use the **Save** button on the Standard toolbar to save and name the document.

Using a Wizard to Create a Document

In Word, *wizards* offer you the same benefits as templates, helping you to create a preformatted document and add your information in the correct places. A wizard includes the added benefit of automation. It walks you through the document creation process, not only letting you make choices about how the document looks but also enabling you to enter some information via dialog boxes rather than skimming through the document to find prompts (areas in a document that cue you to enter information) to fill in.

Task 26: Creating a Document Using a Wizard

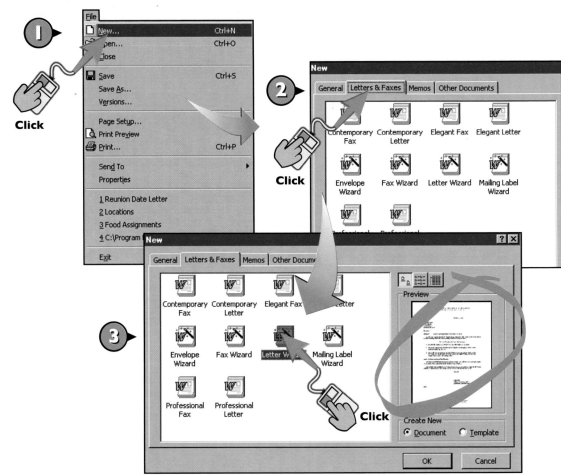

Start Here

Click

Click

Click

1 Choose **File**, **New** (Ctrl+N).

2 Click the tab for the category you want in order to see the templates and wizards in that category.

3 Click the icon for the wizard you want in order to see a preview of it at the right.

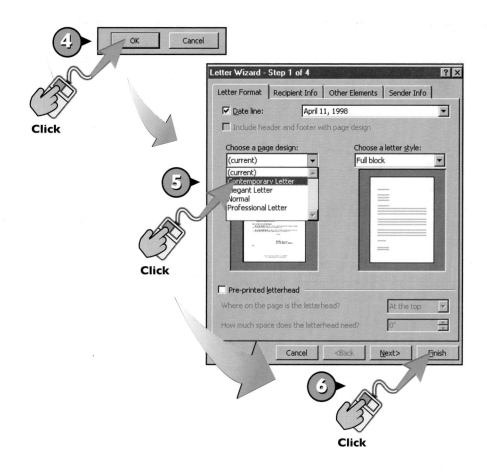

Click

Click

Click

Click

✅ **Finding More Templates and Wizards**
If you want to read a document that explains how you can install and access more templates and wizards in Word, click the **Other Documents** tab in the New dialog box, and then double-click the **More Templates and Wizards** icon.

✅ **Continuing the Wizard**
If the **Office Assistant** pops up after you select a wizard, click one of the choices in its bubble to continue the wizard.

✅ **Clicking Next to Move On**
Some wizards present multiple dialog boxes. After you make your choices in each dialog box, click the **Next** button to continue.

④ ▶ Click **OK** to start the Wizard.

⑤ ▶ Make the choices you want about how the document looks and enter document information in the various tabs of the wizard dialog box.

⑥ ▶ Click **Finish** to close the wizard and create the new document with the options you specified.

Changing Between Page Layout and Normal Views

The view controls how the document appears onscreen and what document and Word features you can see. If you want to focus on plain paragraphs of text, use Normal view. If you want to see how your document will look when printed, choose Page Layout view, the default view in Word. Page Layout view displays a number of things you won't see in Normal view, such as a vertical ruler, clip art pictures and WordArt inserted in the document, and other document features, such as headers and footers or columns.

ⓘ WARNING

The View menu offers other types of views, such as the Outline view. These other views require more knowledge of Word and its features. If you want to try another view, look it up in online Help.

Task 27: Changing Between Page Layout and Normal Views

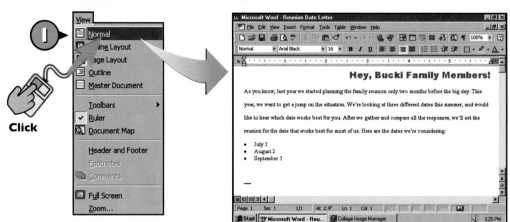

Click

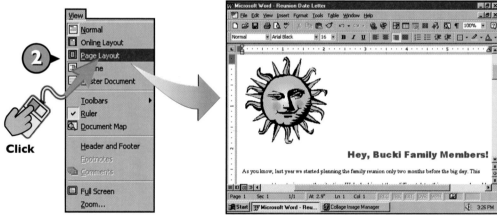

Click

From the Page Layout view, choose **View**, **Normal** to display Normal view.

From the Normal view, choose **View**, **Page Layout** to display Page Layout view.

Task 28: Printing a Document

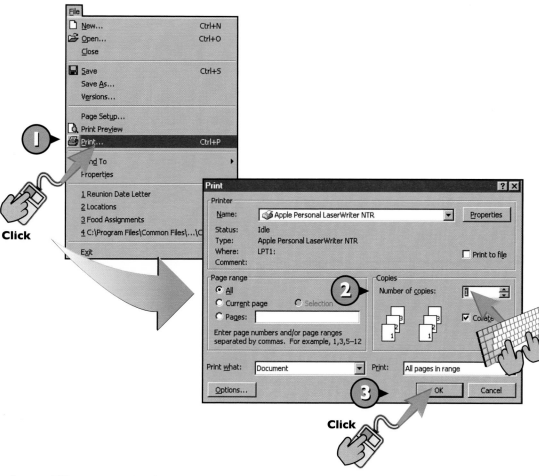

Click

Click

Printing a Document

When you want a paper copy of your document, you need to print it. You can save time by printing multiple copies at once. Make sure your printer is turned on and has paper before you print. If you have trouble printing, check to make sure the printer cable is plugged in all the way.

WARNING
If you just click the **Print** button on the Standard toolbar, Word prints only one copy of the document, using the default print settings.

Finding More Print Option Information
The Print dialog box offers other choices not described in this task, such as the **Collate** check box or the **Pages** text box, which you can use to specify a page to print. To find out how to use other options in the Print dialog box, click the question mark (**?**) button in the dialog box.

I ▶ Choose **File**, **Print** (Ctrl+P).

2 ▶ Type a new value for the **Number of Copies** text box. (It's selected by default.)

3 ▶ Click **OK** to finish the print job.

End Task

PART 2

Tackling Other Tasks with Works 4.5

The Microsoft Works 4.5 program actually offers four different software tools: word processor, spreadsheet, database, and communications. These tools enable you to use your computer to gather and track a number of different types of information: documents, numbers and calculations, lists of information, or information online with bulletin boards. In addition, the Works tools provide your most-needed features, but aren't bogged down with dozens of features you'll never use. So if you want a gentle introduction to a new type of computing task, try it out in Works, using the tasks in this part.

Tasks

Task 1: Starting and Exiting Works

Opening and Closing Works

To access an individual tool in Works, you need to start the Works program itself. Starting Works displays its Task Launcher, which you can use to create a new preformatted document by using a TaskWizard or to select a Works tool to create a blank document. When you've finished working with Works, you can exit Works from within a Works tool or from the Task Launcher.

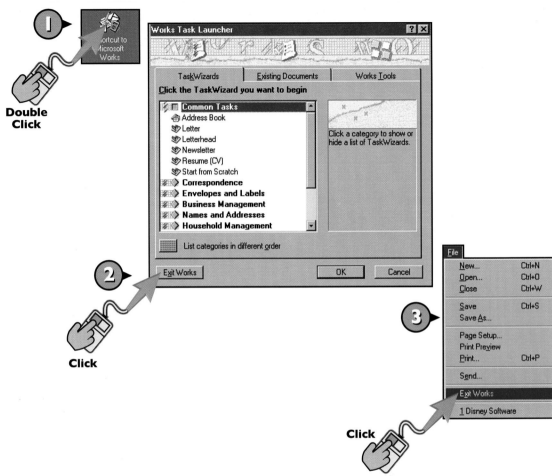

Start Here

1 — Double Click

Double Click

2 — Click

Click

3

Click

✓ **Use the Start Menu**
To use the Start menu to launch Works, click **Start**, point to **Programs, Microsoft Works,** and then click **Microsoft Works.**

1▶ Double-click the **Shortcut to Microsoft Works** shortcut on the Windows Desktop.

2▶ Click the **Exit Works** button to exit Works from the Task Launcher.

3▶ Choose **File**, **Exit Works** from within a Works tool to close the tool and Works.

End Task

Task 2: Redisplaying the Task Launcher

Start Here

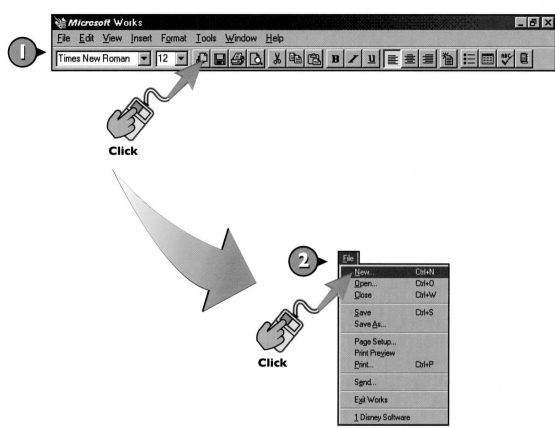

Click

Click

Opening the Task Launcher

After you open or create a file in Works, Task Launcher closes. The Works screen displays the tool (word processor, spreadsheet, database, or communications) for working with that type of file. To start a file using the current tool or another tool, you need to redisplay the Task Launcher, using one of the two methods described in this task.

✔ Displaying Another File

If you have started files in more than one Works tool (leaving each file open), you can switch between the tools. To do so, open the **Window** menu in any Works tool and choose the name of the file to display from the bottom of the menu. Works displays the file in the Works tool you used to create it.

1 ▶ Click the **Task Launcher** button on the Works toolbar.

2 ▶ Choose **File**, **New** (Ctrl+N) from within a Works tool.

End Task

Task 3: Working with the Help Window

Using Works Help

When you're working in a Works tool, you may see that the right side of the screen includes a special Help window. This window lists a menu of Help topics that apply to the Works tool you're using. You can use the Help window to display steps for performing a Works operation, or you can hide the Help window if you want to be able to see and work with more of the open file onscreen.

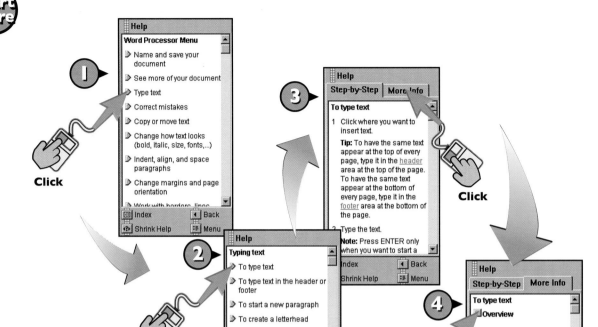

Click

Click

Click

Click

Start Here

✓ **Unhiding Help**
If you don't see the Help window or even the Shrink Help button for hiding and expanding the Help window, choose **Help, Show Help** to redisplay Help.

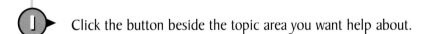

1 ▸ Click the button beside the topic area you want help about.

2 ▸ In the list of tasks that appears, click the button beside the task you want to learn.

3 ▸ After you review the instructions on the **Step-by-Step** tab, click the **More Info** tab.

4 ▸ Click the button beside the topic you would like to review.

Next Step ▸

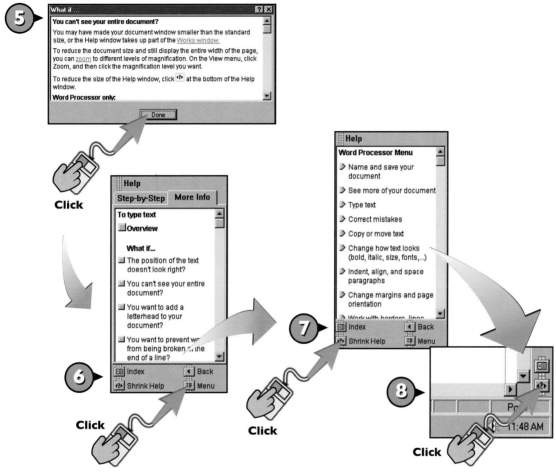

Finding Help About a Topic

Click the **Index** button to display a Help Topics window that has Index and Contents tabs. To find help about a particular topic, type it in the text box at the top of the Index tab and double-click the matching topic in the scrolling list below the text box; or click the **Contents** tab, click the Works tool you need help with, click to open folder icons, and then click a specific topic (denoted by a page icon) to display it in the Help window at the right side of the screen. Click the **Close** button to close the Help Topics window.

Backing Up in Help

Click the **Back** button at the bottom of the Help window to redisplay the previous Help window contents.

5 After you review the information in the window that appears, click **Done** to close it.

6 To redisplay the menu of Help topics (step 1), click the **Menu** button at the bottom of the Help window.

7 To hide the Help window, click the **Shrink Help** button.

8 To redisplay the **Help** window, click (again) the **Shrink Help** button at the lower-right corner of the screen.

Task 4: Creating a New Document with a TaskWizard

Using a TaskWizard to Make a Document

Like Word 97, you use the Works word processor to create text-based documents such as letters, resumes, flyers, and certificates. If you want a leg up starting a new document file, you can use a TaskWizard, which designs the document and prompts you where to enter your information. Some of the TaskWizards appear under more than one category in the TaskWizards tab of the Task Launcher.

✓ **Other Works Tools**
If you need to calculate numbers, use the spreadsheet tool, covered in Tasks 8 through 24. If you need to track and sort a list of entries, use the database tool, covered in Tasks 25 through 39. There are TaskWizards for creating both spreadsheet and database files.

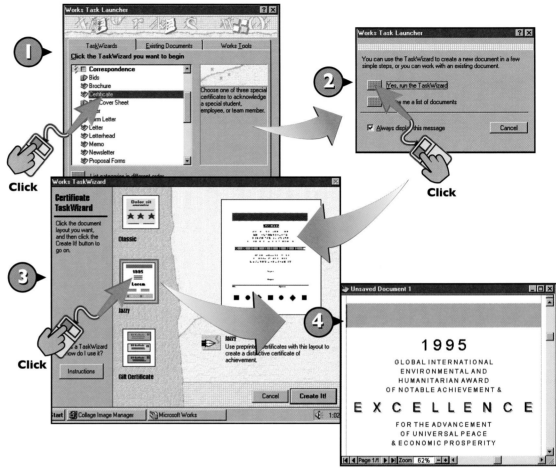

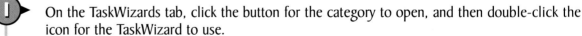

1. On the TaskWizards tab, click the button for the category to open, and then double-click the icon for the TaskWizard to use.

2. Click the **Yes, Run the TaskWizard** button.

3. Click the preview for the document design to use and then click **Create It!**

4. Edit the new document (see Task 6).

Task 5: Creating a Blank Document in the Word Processor Tool

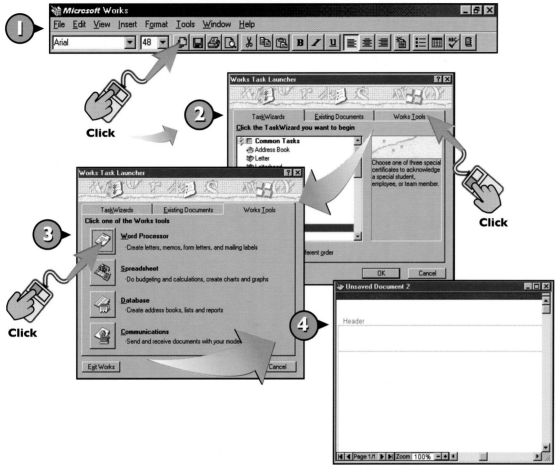

Start Here

Click

Click

Click

① Click the **Task Launcher** button or choose **File**, **New** to redisplay the Task Launcher if needed.

② Click the **Works Tools** tab.

③ Click the **Word Processor** button.

④ Edit the new document (see Task 6).

Opening a Blank Document

If there's no TaskWizard that creates the type of document you need, you can create a blank document to start from scratch.

✓ **Dismissing First-Time Help**

If the First-Time Help window appears when you're creating a new document, you can click **OK** to bypass it. In fact, any time you see a First-Time Help window, you can click one of its choices to get Help about the operation you're attempting or click **OK** to bypass the dialog box.

End Task

Creating and Changing Text

In the Works word processor, you use the same techniques to move the insertion point and edit text as you do in Word 97. This task reviews the most critical techniques. See Tasks 3 and 5 through 10 to learn more about editing techniques, including how to select text for editing and formatting.

⚠ WARNING

If you're typing and you get an unexpected result, you may have accidentally pressed the **Ctrl** key or **Alt** key instead of the **Shift** key. Try pressing **Ctrl+Z** to undo the action or press **Esc** once or twice to close any dialog box or menu that appears.

Task 6: Entering and Editing Document Content

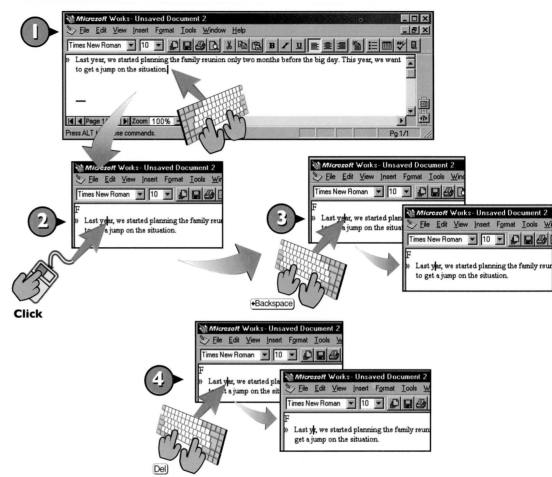

Start Here

Click

←Backspace

Del

1 ▶ Type your first paragraph, letting text wrap to the next line as needed at the right margin.

2 ▶ Click or press an arrow key to move the insertion point where needed.

3 ▶ Press the **Backspace** key to remove the character to the left of the insertion point.

4 ▶ Press the **Delete** key to remove the character to the right of the insertion point.

Next Step

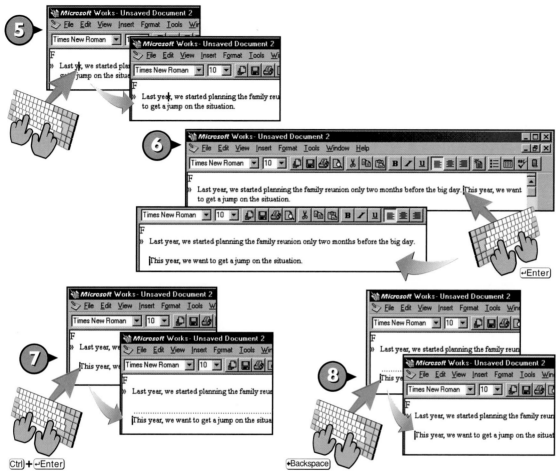

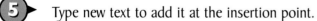

Ctrl+↵Enter

←Backspace

5 ▶ Type new text to add it at the insertion point.

6 ▶ Press **Enter** once (or twice to insert a blank line) to start a new paragraph at the insertion point.

7 ▶ Click to position the insertion point where you want to start a new page and press **Ctrl+Enter**.

8 ▶ Click after a page or paragraph break or blank line, then press **Backspace** to delete it.

✔ **Controlling Page Breaks**
If you add or remove a large amount of text in a document, Works automatically inserts and removes soft (automatic) page breaks. You can insert a *hard page break* (also called a *manual page break*) where you need it, as described in step 7.

End Task

Task 7: Changing Basic Text Formatting

Formatting Text

You guessed it. You also can use many of the same techniques for formatting text that you use in Word 97 in the Works word processor. This task freshens up those skills. See Tasks 11 through 14 and 17 to learn more about formatting techniques.

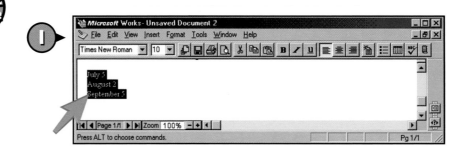

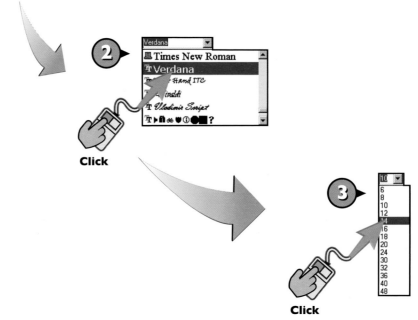

Click

Click

✓ Selecting Text
You must select text to apply formatting to it. The fastest way to make a selection is to drag over it with the mouse, holding down the left mouse button as you drag.

✓ Opening a Drop-Down List
Remember, to open a drop-down list on a toolbar or in a dialog box, click the drop-down list arrow (the downward pointing arrow to the right) for the list.

1 Select the text to format.

2 Open the **Font Name** drop-down list and click a new font to apply it.

3 Open the **Font Size** drop-down list and click a new size to apply it.

Next Step

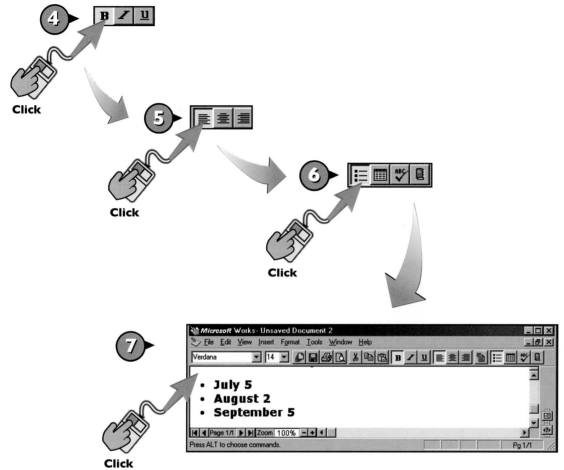

4 To apply or remove boldface, italic, or underlining, click the **Bold**, **Italic**, or **Underline** button.

5 To select a new paragraph alignment, click the **Left Align**, **Center Align**, or **Right Align** button.

6 To apply or remove bullets to the selection, click the **Bullets** button.

7 Click outside the selection to see the formatting changes you've made.

✅ **Applying an Easy Format**
Works offers Easy Formats—predefined formatting combinations that you can apply to a selection. To apply an Easy Format to a selection, choose **Format, Easy Formats**. Scroll through the list in the Easy Formats dialog box, click an Easy Format to see a sample of it, and click **Apply**.

✅ **Performing More Formatting**
The Format menu offers additional formatting choices, enabling you to do things such as adding shading and a border to a paragraph.

Using a TaskWizard to Create a Spreadsheet

You use the Works spreadsheet tool primarily to work with numerical values and labels for them. After you enter your values, you can enter a formula to calculate the data. The spreadsheet tool stores your values in a spreadsheet file. You can use a TaskWizard to create a spreadsheet that already contains labels, formulas, and formatting. After you create a spreadsheet from a TaskWizard, all you need to do is enter your values.

✓ Finding a Spreadsheet TaskWizard

The Task Launcher identifies spreadsheet TaskWizards with a calculator and ledger icon. Other icons identify TaskWizards for the word processor or database tools.

Task 8: Creating a New Spreadsheet with a TaskWizard

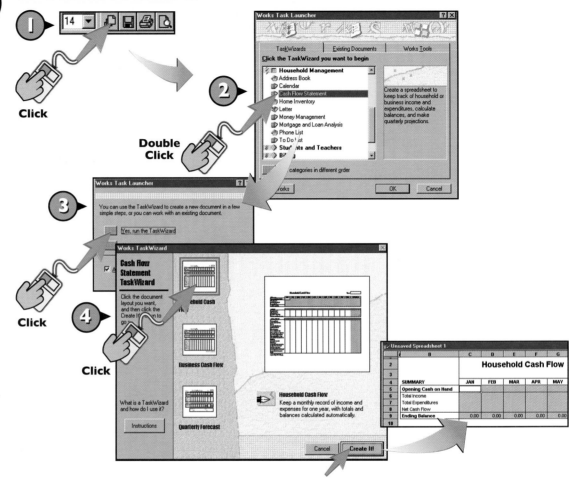

1. Click the **Task Launcher** button to redisplay the Task Launcher.

2. On the TaskWizards tab, click the button for the category to open and double-click the icon for the TaskWizard to use.

3. Click the **Yes, Run the TaskWizard** button.

4. Click the preview for the document design to use, and then click **Create It!** You can now edit the new document (see Tasks 10–12).

Task 9: Creating a Blank Spreadsheet in the Spreadsheet Tool

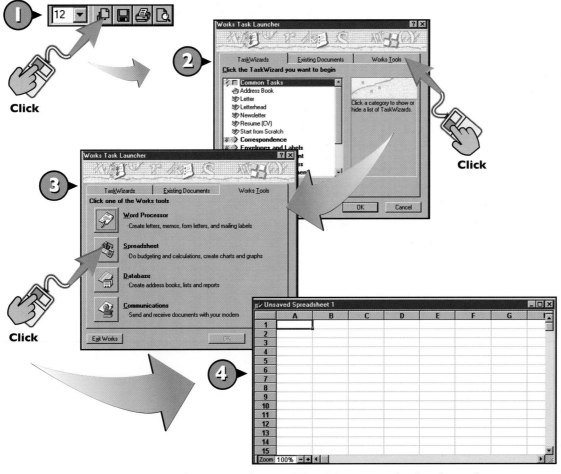

Click

Click

Click

Opening a Blank Spreadsheet

If there's no TaskWizard that creates the type of spreadsheet you need, you can create a blank spreadsheet and start from scratch.

Click the **Task Launcher** button or choose **File**, **New** to redisplay the Task Launcher if needed.

Click the **Works Tools** tab.

Click the **Spreadsheet** button.

Edit the new spreadsheet (see Tasks 10–12).

End Task

Task 10: Entering Text in a Spreadsheet

Creating Spreadsheet Text

Each spreadsheet consists of a grid of rows and columns that intersect to form cells. You type each spreadsheet entry into a separate cell. A black cell selector highlights the current cell, which is the cell where your entry will appear. The spreadsheet tool treats text entries (also called labels for your data) differently from numerical and date entries. For starters, text lines up at the left side of the cell. The spreadsheet automatically inserts a left double prime (") to the left of a label entry to identify the entry as text. The spreadsheet won't calculate cells containing text because it can only calculate values.

✓ **Finishing Any Cell Entry**
No matter whether you're entering text or a number (value), you can finish the entry by clicking the **Check Mark** button on the entry bar, by pressing **Tab**, or by pressing **Enter**.

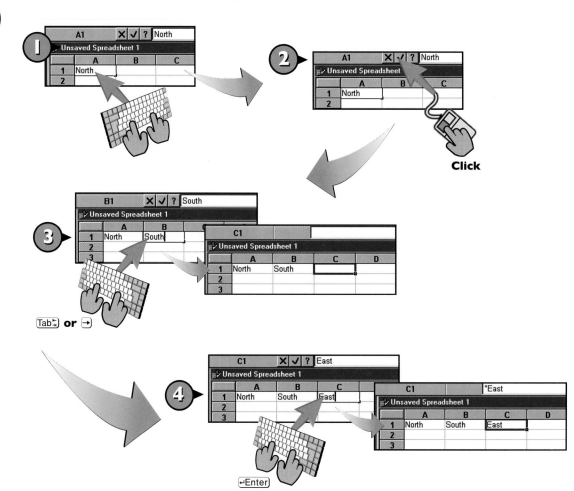

Click

Tab⇥ or →

↵Enter

1 Type a label entry in the current cell.

2 Click the **Check Mark** button on the entry bar to finish the entry.

3 Press **Tab** or the **right arrow** button to move one cell right or the **down arrow** button to move one cell down.

4 Type another entry and press **Tab** to move to the next cell or **Enter** to finish it.

Task 11: Entering Numbers and Dates in a Spreadsheet

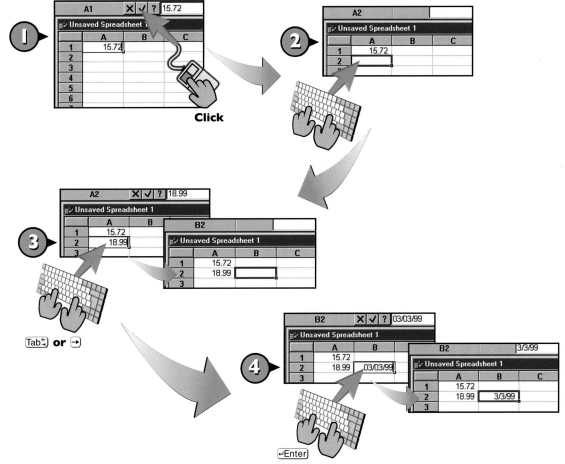

Click

[Tab⇆] **or** ⊡

←Enter

Typing Numbers and Dates in a Spreadsheet

Numbers form the core of every spreadsheet because spreadsheet programs exist to calculate them. When you enter a number in a cell, it lines up at the right side of the cell. Dates do, too. When you enter a number, type a period to indicate the decimal point, as well as any digits to the right of the decimal point. You can apply special formats to cells with numbers, such as how many decimal points display and whether a dollar sign is included. See Task 22 to learn about number formatting.

---

1 Type a number entry in the current cell and click the **Check Mark** button on the entry bar to finish the entry.

2 Press **Tab** or **right arrow** button to move one cell right or the **down arrow** button to move one cell down.

3 Type another entry and press **Tab** to finish it and move one cell to the right.

4 Type a date and press **Enter** to finish it.

✓ Wide Cell Entries

If a number you enter into a cell displays as a series of pound signs (####), that means the entry is too wide. (Text entries just spill over the adjacent right cell.) You can change the column width to display the full number (see Task 21).

Task 12: Moving Around in the Spreadsheet

Navigating to a Cell

The cell reference (or cell address) identifies each cell in the spreadsheet. The cell's column letter and row number combine to form its reference—that is, the cell in row 4 of column **B** is cell **B4**. The left side of the entry bar (below the toolbar in the spreadsheet) displays the reference for the current (selected) cell. Entries or changes you make appear in the current cell. This task shows you how to move around the spreadsheet to select a cell with either the mouse or keyboard in preparation for your entries and edits.

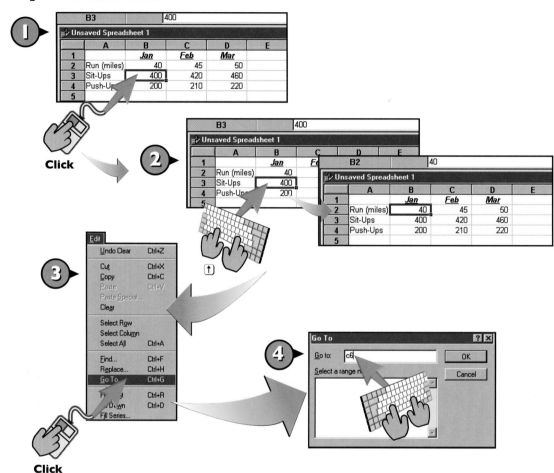

Start Here

Click

Click

✓ **Moving with the Keyboard**
Press **Ctrl+Home** to go to cell **A1**. Press **Ctrl+End** to display the last cell in the spreadsheet containing data. Pressing **Home** or **End** goes to the first or last cell in the row that contains data, respectively.

1 ▸ Click any cell to select it.

2 ▸ Press an arrow key to move one column or row in the direction of the arrow.

3 ▸ Choose **Edit**, **Go To** (Ctrl+G).

4 ▸ Type the cell reference for the cell to select in the Go To text box and click **OK**.

End Task

Task 13: Selecting a Range, Row, or Column

Start
Here

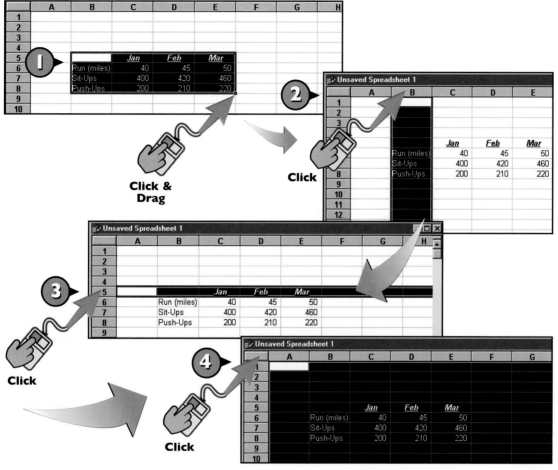

Click &
Drag

Click

Click

Click

Making a Larger Selection

For some operations, you may need to select more than a single cell. If you want to give the same formatting to a group of adjacent cells, called a range, you can select the whole range rather than formatting the cells one by one. To insert or delete a row or column in the spreadsheet, you need to select an entire row or column.

✓ **Addressing the Range**
The range reference combines the cell reference for the upper-left cell in the range with the lower-right cell in the range, separated by a colon. If a range spans from cell **B3** to cell **D8**, the range reference is **B3:D8**.

✓ **The Keyboard**
Press and hold the **Shift** key and press one or more arrow keys to select a range.

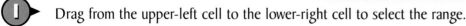

1 ▶ Drag from the upper-left cell to the lower-right cell to select the range.

2 ▶ Click a column letter to select the entire column.

3 ▶ Click a row number to select the entire row.

4 ▶ Click the gray button above the row row number to select the entire spreadsheet.

End
Task

Using Easy Calc to Enter a Formula

A formula performs calculations on the values you've entered into spreadsheet cells or on other numbers you enter into the formula. Each formula begins with an equal sign and uses the mathematical operators + (addition), - (subtraction), * (multiplication), and / (division). For example, =A3+52 adds 52 to whatever value you entered in cell A3. Or =B2*B3 multiplies the values in those cells. Formulas also can use functions, which serve as shorthand for more complicated formulas and enable you to perform a calculation on a range. For example, you can use the Sum function to total a range, as in =SUM(B2:B4). Rather than learning all the ins and outs of formulas and functions, you can use Easy Calc to help you build a formula.

Task 14: Building a Basic Formula with Easy Calc

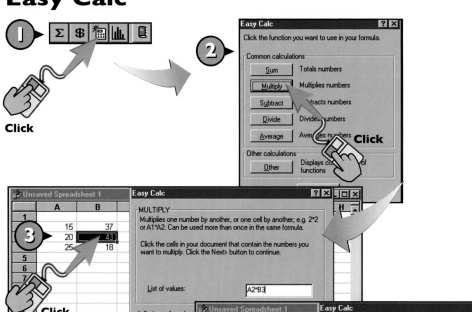

Click

Click

Click

Click & Drag

 Click the **Easy Calc** button on the toolbar.

 Click the type of calculation you would like to perform.

 If prompted to enter cell references in the formula, click each one to include in the spreadsheet.

 If prompted to enter a range reference in the formula, drag over the range in the spreadsheet.

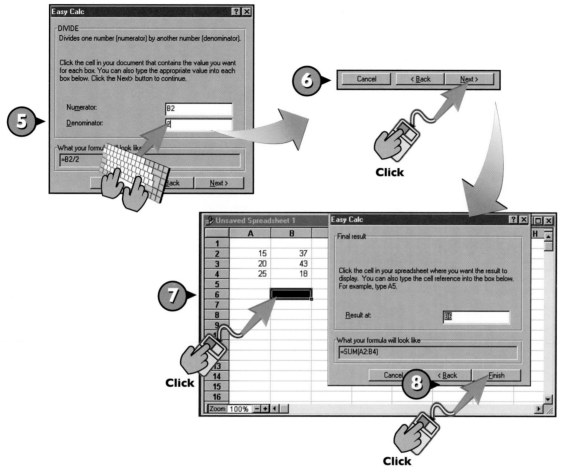

Click

Click

Click

WARNING
By default, the spreadsheet tool multiplies and divides first and then adds and subtracts. It does not work from left to right as you would. To control the calculation order, use parentheses. Works calculates the information in the innermost pair of parentheses first, and then works outward. For example, Works would calculate the formula =5+7*(2+2) as 33, whereas the result would be 26 if you calculated from left to right.

Displaying a Formula
The cell that holds the formula displays the calculated formula result, not the formula itself. When you select a cell containing a formula, the formula appears in the entry bar.

⑤ If prompted to enter either a number or a cell reference, type the number or click to select a cell.

⑥ Click **Next**.

⑦ Click the cell that you want to hold the formula.

⑧ Click **Finish**.

Task 15: Using a Function for a Calculation

Calculating with a Function

Functions are predefined formulas that perform a more complex calculation. A function performs its calculations on the arguments you specify. Each argument may be a value you enter or a cell or range reference. The Works spreadsheet offers dozens of functions. You do not need to remember each function and the arguments it requires. Instead, you can insert the function, and Works prompts you for the proper arguments.

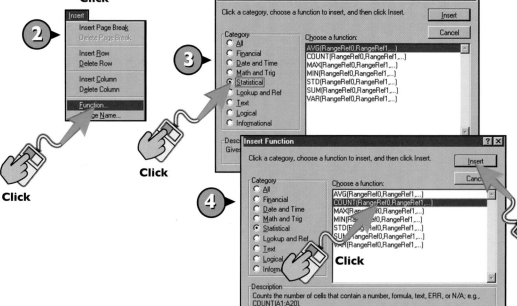

✓ **Summing Up Cells**
You can click the AutoSum button to enter a formula that sums the values above or to the left of the current cell.

✓ **Canceling an Entry**
You can press **Esc** at any time to cancel a cell entry, function, or formula you're entering.

1 ▶ Click to select the cell where you want to insert the formula with a function.

2 ▶ Choose **Insert**, **Function**.

3 ▶ Click the **Category** that contains the function to use.

4 ▶ Click the function to use in the **Choose a Function** list and click **Insert**.

Next Step ▶

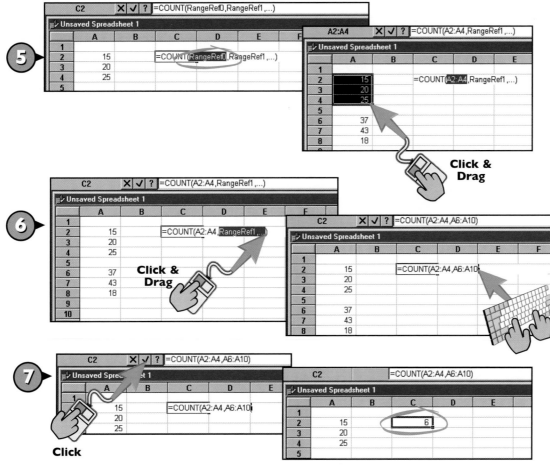

WARNING
Be sure to enter arguments just as prompted by Works. For example, if an argument calls for a percentage but you specify a cell that doesn't display the intended percentage, the calculation results will be wrong. You also may need to divide a percentage rate by 12 (as in 7.5%/12) to yield a monthly rate. If you specify an argument entry that won't work at all, such as entering a range when Works expects a single value or cell reference, Works displays an error message.

Entering Needed Arguments
Works inserts the arguments within parentheses and uses a comma to separate arguments. If there's an ellipsis (...) after the last argument, you can enter as many arguments as you want, separating each with a comma. If there's no ellipsis, enter only those arguments specified by the inserted function formula.

Click & Drag

Click & Drag

Click

5 ▶ Type an entry, click to select one cell, or drag to select a range to fill in the first highlighted (by default) argument.

6 ▶ Drag over the next argument and type the next value, cell, or range reference to fill it in. Repeat this process for subsequent arguments.

7 ▶ Click the **Check Mark** button on the entry bar to finish entering the formula.

End Task

Task 16: Editing a Cell

Changing Cell Content

As information changes, you may find that you need to adjust the entries on your spreadsheet. Your electronic spreadsheet is much easier to update than a paper ledger. You can either completely retype a cell entry, or you can edit a longer entry, such as a formula, to correct it.

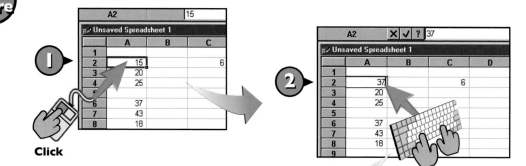

Click

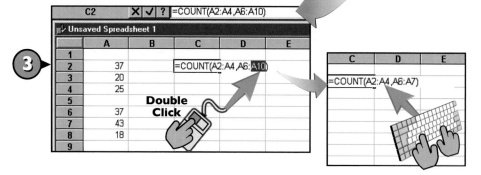

Double Click

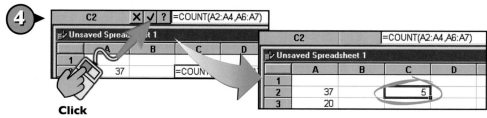

Click

✓ Editing in the Entry Bar

You can click the cell to edit and then click in the entry bar to make your changes there.

① Click the cell to edit.

② Type the new entry and click the **Check Mark** button on the entry bar or press **Enter**.

③ Double-click a cell that holds a longer entry, and then drag over the portion of the entry to edit and type your changes.

④ Click the **Check Mark** button on the entry bar or press **Enter** to finish.

Task 17: Undoing a Change

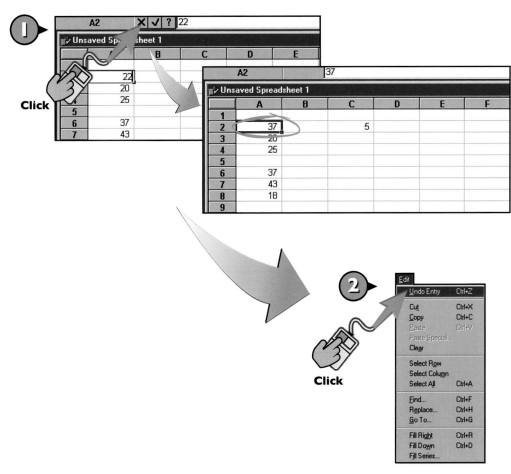

Click

Click

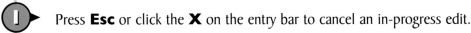

Using Undo

Editing and formatting your spreadsheet can be an imperfect process. You may change an entry or formula and find you've introduced an inaccuracy. Or you might be experimenting with the look of your spreadsheet and decide you don't like a formatting change you just made. You can cancel or undo an entry or change it, if needed.

⚠ WARNING

Unlike Word 97, which enables you to undo multiple previous changes, Works only enables you to undo the change you just made. So you must use the Undo command immediately in Works.

✓ Undoing in Other Tools

The Works word processor and database tools also offer the Undo command. The communications tool does not, however. Ctrl+Z is the shortcut combination for the Undo command.

---

1 ▶ Press **Esc** or click the **X** on the entry bar to cancel an in-progress edit.

2 ▶ To undo the previous change, choose **Edit**, **Undo Entry**. The command changes based on the last change you made.

Adding Attributes to Cells

To emphasize certain cells in the spreadsheet, you can change their formatting. You can start out by applying **boldface**, *italic*, or underlining to the text labels you enter in a spreadsheet to call attention to those labels.

✓ **Removing Attributes**
To remove boldface, italic, or underlining you've previously applied to a cell, select the cell and click the **Bold**, **Italic**, or **Underline** button to remove the formatting.

✓ **Keyboard Shortcuts for Formatting**
You can press **Ctrl+B** to apply or remove boldface, **Ctrl+I** to apply or remove italic, and **Ctrl+U** to apply or remove underlining.

Task 18: Adding Boldface, Italic, or Underlining to a Selection

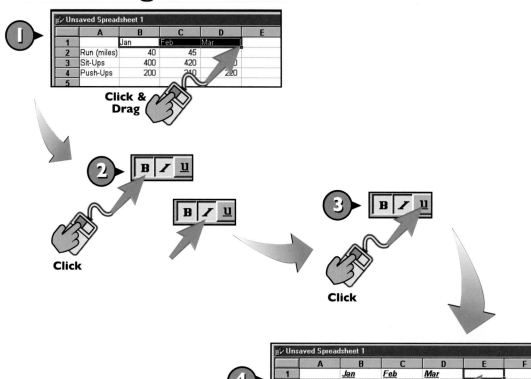

Start Here

Click & Drag

Click

Click

Click

Click

1. Select the cell or range to format.

2. Click the **Bold** button, and then click the **Italic** button.

3. Click the **Underline** button.

4. Click outside the selection to see your changes.

End Task

Task 19: Choosing a New Font and Size for a Selection

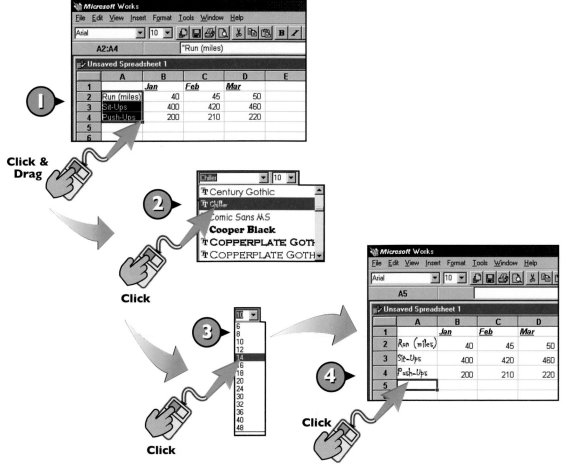

Click & Drag

Click

Click

Click

Click

Changing the Cell Font and Size

You can change the font (letter style) used by a cell's contents or increase the font size. When you increase the font size, the spreadsheet tool automatically increases or decreases the row height as needed. However, it does not increase the column width, which means your text entries might get cut off at the right (if the next cell to the right contains an entry), or number or formula entries might display as a string of pound signs (########). To redisplay the full entry, you can increase the column width, as described in Task 21, "Changing Column Width or Row Height."

① Select the cell or range to format.

② Open the **Font Name** drop-down list and click a new font to apply it.

③ Open the **Font Size** drop-down list and click a new size to apply it.

④ Click outside the selection to see your changes.

✓ **AutoFormatting a Spreadsheet**
The Works spreadsheet offers AutoFormats — predefined formatting combinations you can apply to a selection (choose **Format, AutoFormat**).

Task 20: Changing Cell Alignment

Aligning Cell Contents

In word processors, you can change how paragraphs line up relative to the left and right margins (horizontal alignment). In the spreadsheet tool, you control how cell entries line up relative to the borders of the cell, including the top and bottom borders (called the vertical alignment). In addition, the spreadsheet's **Alignment tab in the Format Cells dialog box** offers some special formatting choices, described elsewhere in this task. The General alignment changes the cell's horizontal alignment depending on the type of entry (lining up text to the left and numbers to the right).

✓ **Using the Format Cells Dialog**

After you display the Format Cells dialog box, you can click any of its tabs and change other formatting settings before clicking **OK** to close the dialog box and apply your choices.

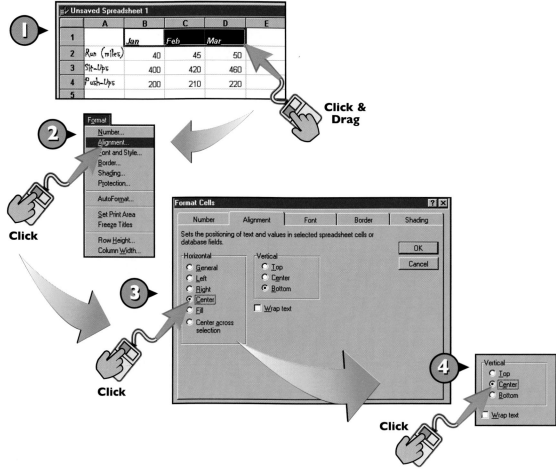

Start Here

Click & Drag

Click

Click

Click

1️⃣ Select the cell or range to format.

2️⃣ Choose **Format**, **Alignment**.

3️⃣ Click a choice in the **Horizontal** area of the Alignment tab to determine the horizontal alignment.

4️⃣ Click a choice in the **Vertical** area of the Alignment tab to determine the vertical alignment.

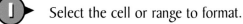

Next Step

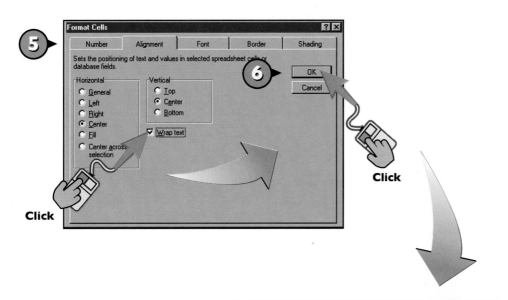

Click

Click

Click

Click

Using Other Alignments

The **Fill** choice repeats the cell entry to fill the cell's width. The **Center Across Selection** choice centers the entry in the first cell of a range across the entire range. That is, if you want to center a lengthy cell entry across three cells, select a range that includes the entry plus two cells to the right before applying this choice. The **Wrap Text** choice divides a lengthy cell entry into several lines within the cell and increases the row height so that all of the entry can display in the cell.

Using Alignment Buttons

You can quickly change the selection's horizontal alignment by clicking the **Left Align, Center Align,** or **Right Align button** on the spreadsheet tool's toolbar.

---

5 ▶ Click to check the **Wrap Text** check box if you need to wrap long entries in the selection.

6 ▶ Click the **OK** button to close the dialog box and apply your alignment settings.

7 ▶ Click outside the selection to see your changes.

End Task

Task 21: Changing Column Width or Row Height

Adjusting Columns and Rows

The last several tasks mentioned that an entry or formatting change can cause a cell to be cut off at the right or displayed as pound signs because it can't fit in the cell. This task presents the fix for that problem and other situations where you might want to change the width of columns and the height of rows.

✓ **Fine-Tuning Rows and Columns**

The Row Height and Column Width dialog boxes work identically. In addition to specifying a precise column width (in characters) or row height (in points), you can click the **Standard** button in either dialog box to close the box and return the row height or column width to the default. Click the **Best Fit** button in either dialog box to close the box and size the selected columns (or rows) to fit the widest (or tallest) entry in the column (or row).

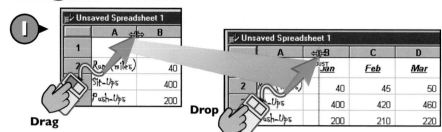

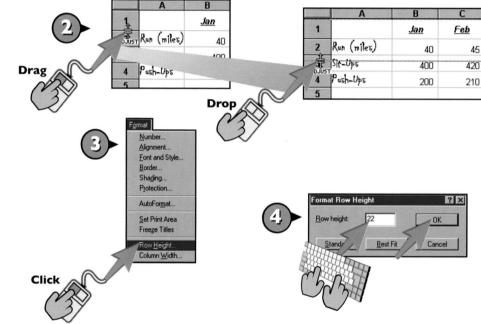

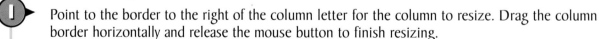

Start Here

1 Point to the border to the right of the column letter for the column to resize. Drag the column border horizontally and release the mouse button to finish resizing.

2 Point to the border below the row number for the row to resize. Drag the row border vertically and release the mouse to finish resizing.

3 Alternately, click a cell in the column or row to resize and choose **Format**, **Column Width** or **Format**, **Row Height**.

4 Enter the new column width or row height and click **OK**.

End Task

Task 22: Changing the Number Format

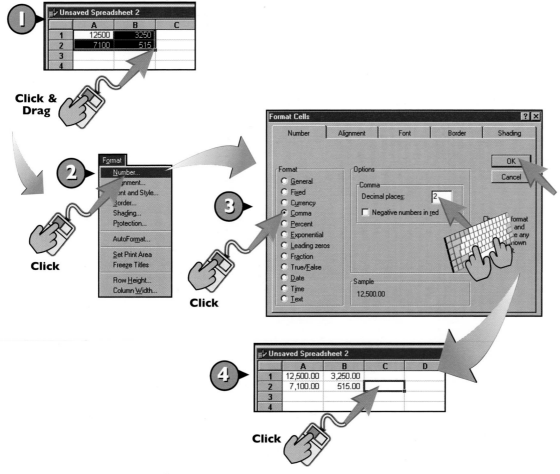

Click & Drag

Click

Click

Click

Click

Adjusting Number Display

Numbers can often require special types of formatting not found with text. For example, you may want to display a decimal point and two decimal places with a value, even when you enter a round number (as in 25.00). Or you may want to have your spreadsheet display decimal values as fractions ($1\frac{1}{4}$ rather than 1.25, for example). You accomplish these special number formatting feats and others by applying a number format to a cell.

1 ▶ Select the cell or range to format.

2 ▶ Choose **Format**, **Number**.

3 ▶ Click the number format to apply in the Format list. If format Options appear, such as entering a number of decimal places, make your changes and click **OK**.

4 ▶ Click outside the selection to see your changes.

 Number Formatting On-the-Fly
You can apply the Currency and Percent formats as you type by entering a dollar sign before the value (as in $25) or a percent sign after the value (as in 25%).

End Task

Shading and Outlining a Range

If a selection contains particularly significant or unique entries, you can call maximum attention to the selection by adding a border around it and some shading within it. You accomplish both of these tasks with the Format Cells dialog box.

Task 23: Adding a Border and Shading to a Range

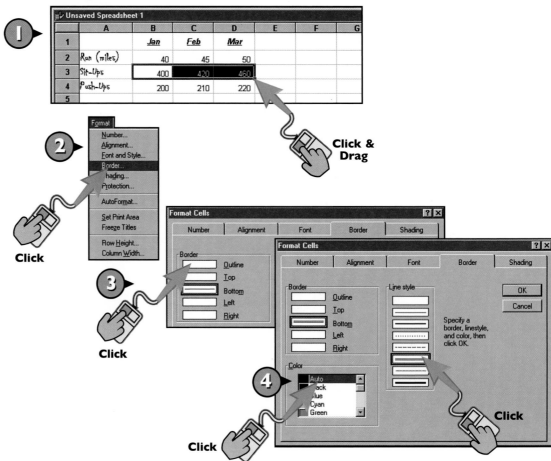

Start Here

Click & Drag

Click

Click

Click

Click

✅ **Shading a Range Only**
If you want to apply shading but no border to a cell, you can save a little time by choosing **Format, Shading** to go directly to the Shading tab of the Format Cells dialog box.

1 Select the cell or range to format.

2 Choose **Format, Border**.

3 In the **Border** area, click the **Outline** choice or any combination of the other four choices.

4 Click a **Line Style** choice and click a **Color** choice.

Next Step

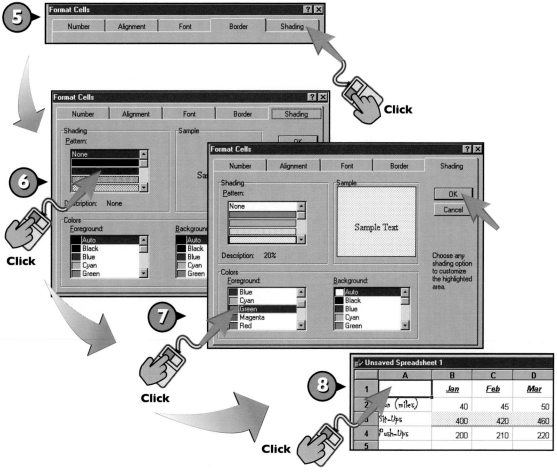

5 ► Click the **Shading** tab.

6 ► Click the **Pattern** you want to apply.

7 ► Click a new **Foreground** or **Background** color (or both) and click **OK**.

8 ► Click outside the selection to see your changes.

✅ Removing Borders or Shading

Click the blank **Line Style** on the Border tab and then click one or more **Border** choices to remove a previously applied border. Or click the **None Pattern** on the Shading tab to remove previously applied shading.

Task 24: Creating a Chart

Charting Values

While your spreadsheet entries have all the precision you want, they don't necessarily clarify how the entries relate. You can more clearly see trends or how the different values compare by charting your data. You can choose one of 12 different chart types for your chart.

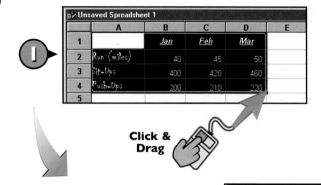

Click & Drag

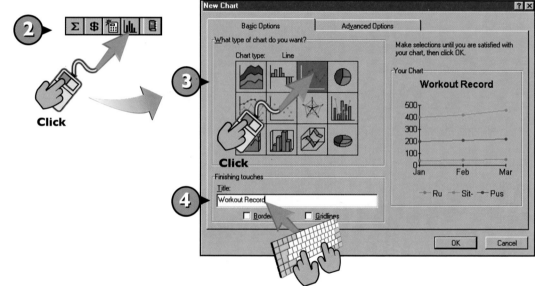

Click

Click

✅ Using Charting Commands

A chart you create appears in its own window. When the chart window is open onscreen, the Format and Tools menus change to offer commands for working with charts.

1 ▶ Select the range to chart, including row or column text that identifies your entries.

2 ▶ Click the **New Chart** button or choose **Tools**, **Create New Chart**.

3 ▶ On the **Basic Options** tab, click the chart type you want. A preview appears at the right.

4 ▶ Enter a name to display on the chart in the **Title** text box.

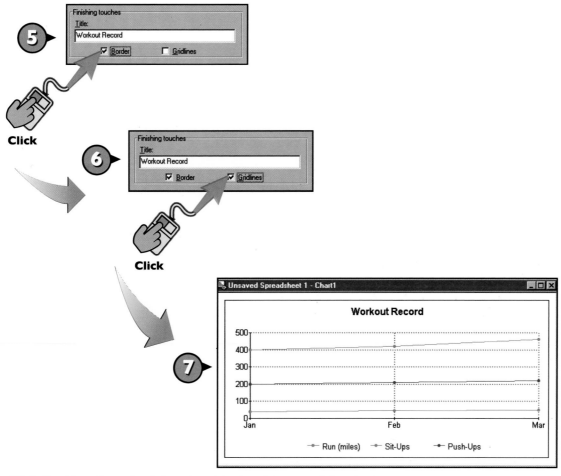

Finishing touches

Title:
Workout Record

☑ Border   ☐ Gridlines

Click

Finishing touches

Title:
Workout Record

☑ Border   ☑ Gridlines

Click

Unsaved Spreadsheet 1 - Chart1

Workout Record

Run (miles)   Sit-Ups   Push-Ups

5 ▸ Click the **Border** check box to add a border around the chart.

6 ▸ Click the **Gridlines** check box to add gridlines to set off the charted data and then click **OK**.

7 ▸ You can then work with the chart as needed.

✓ **Viewing a Chart**
After you add one or more charts to the spreadsheet and save the spreadsheet, you can redisplay any chart at any time. To do so, choose **View, Chart** and double-click the chart to redisplay in the list.

End Task

Task 25: Creating a New Database with a TaskWizard

Using a TaskWizard to Make a Database

You use the Works database tool to keep and organize lists of information. A database stores information in records and fields. For example, if you create an address book database, all the information about each person is a *record*, and each individual piece of information within a record (like the last name) is a *field*. You can use a TaskWizard to create a database with already defined fields so that you can begin entering records.

✓ **Finding a Database TaskWizard**
The Task Launcher identifies database TaskWizards with an address card file icon. Other icons identify TaskWizards for the word processor or spreadsheet tools.

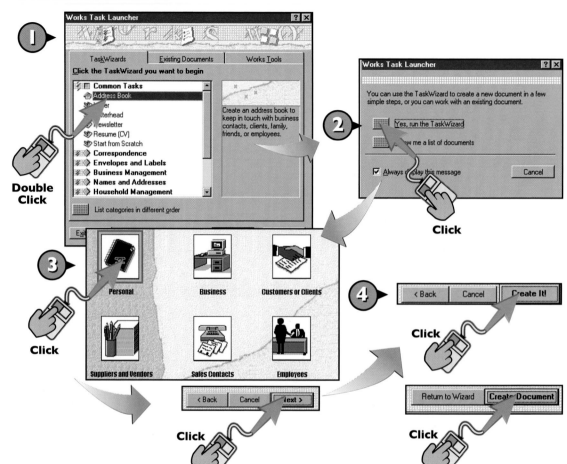

1 ▶ In the Task Launcher, click the **TaskWizards** tab, click the button for the category to open, and then double-click the icon for the TaskWizard to use.

2 ▶ Click the **Yes, Run the TaskWizard** button.

3 ▶ Click the preview for the document design to use and click **Next**. Review the information about the database fields in the next screen and click **Next**.

4 ▶ Click **Create It!** and then click **Create Document** to finish.

Task 26: Filling in New Records in Form View

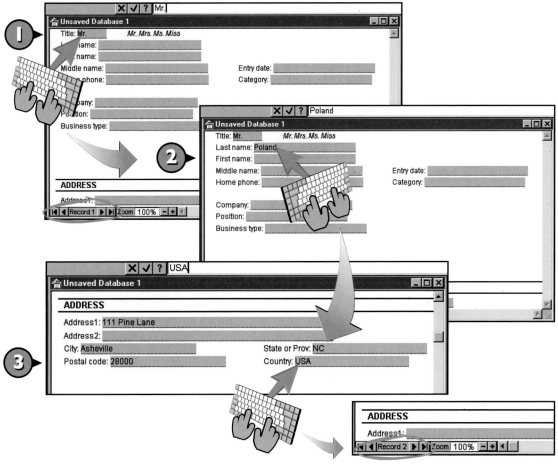

 Type the information for the first field and press **Tab** to select the next field.

 Continue typing entries and pressing **Tab** to move to the next field.

 Press **Tab** after you fill in the last field to complete the current record and start a new one.

Using Form View to Enter Records

After you use a TaskWizard to create a database, the data form appears and displays all the fields in the database. The data form is empty because the database contains no data until you enter some. The data form displays the fields in a spacious form with one record (all the fields for one entry) in a single page. The data form makes it easy to enter and review data record by record because the screen isn't cluttered with other records.

Finding the Active Field

The field that's ready to accept an entry (the selected field) appears in a darker gray than the other fields. To go back to a previous field, click that field, press the **left arrow** key, or **Shift+Tab**. You can then simply type a new entry for the field.

Task 27: Creating a Blank Database with the Database Tool

Starting a Database from Scratch

Most of the database TaskWizards include a lot of fields—often more fields than you need. If there's no TaskWizard that creates a database with all the fields you need or if you want to create a simpler database with fewer fields, you can create a blank database from scratch.

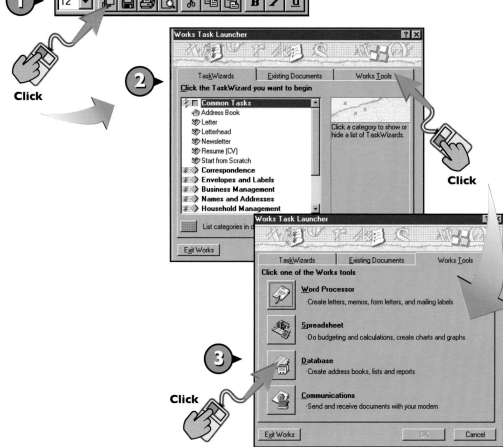

Bypassing First-Time Help

If the First-Time Help window appears after step 3, click **OK** to bypass it. In fact, any time you see a First-Time Help window, you can click one of its choices to get Help about the operation you're attempting, or click **OK** to bypass the dialog box.

1 Click the **Task Launcher** button to redisplay the Task Launcher if needed.

2 Click the **Works Tools** tab.

3 Click the **Database** button.

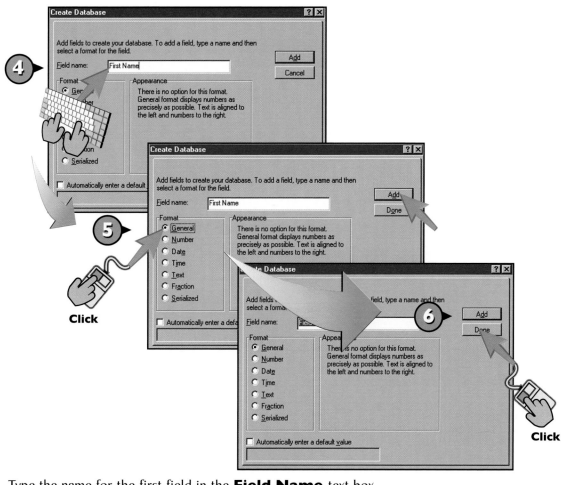

Click

4 ▶ Type the name for the first field in the **Field Name** text box.

5 ▶ If needed, click the field type for the new field under **Format** and click **Add** to add the field.

6 ▶ Repeat steps 4 and 5 to add as many fields as you want; click **Done** to close the Create Database dialog box.

✅ **Determining the Right Format**
For entries that contain only letters (such as names), use the **General** format. If an entry contains both numbers and special characters, such as a phone number, choose the **Text** format.

Using the List View to Enter Records

After you create a blank database with the Database tool, the data list appears and displays fields added in the database, as well as rows for multiple records. The data list is initially empty because the database contains no data until you enter some. Each row in a data list contains a single record. The compact list format enables you to display multiple records on a single page. In the List view, you can review multiple records without having to move back and forth between them.

Task 28: Filling in New Records in List View

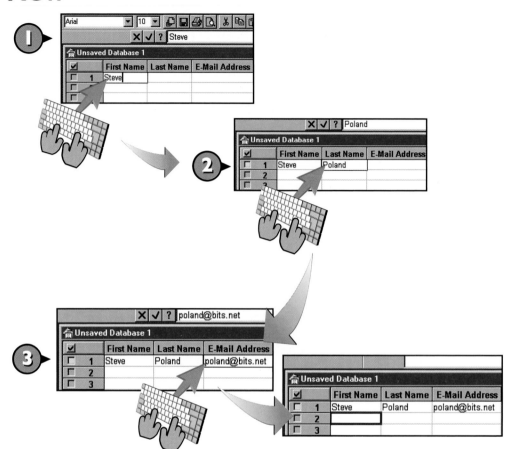

Start Here

Type the information for the first field and press **Tab** to select the next field.

Continue typing entries and pressing **Tab** to move to the next field.

Press **Tab** after you fill in the last field to complete the current record, moving the cell selector to the first field in the next record.

✓ **Finding the Active Field**

The field that's ready to accept an entry (the selected field) has a heavy cell selector border around it, just like in a Works spreadsheet.

End Task

Task 29: Changing Between Form View and List View

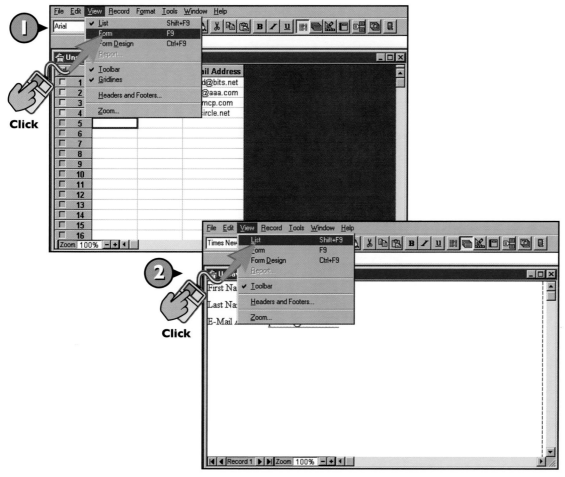

Click

Click

Choosing Form View or List View in the Database

Your preference alone dictates whether you need to enter and work with records in the data form (Form view) or data list (List view). You can easily switch to the view you need.

 Choose **View**, **Form** (F9) to change from the List view to the Form view.

 Choose **View**, **List** (Shift+F9) to change from the Form view to the List view.

 Printing a Database View
When you print your database file, Works prints the current view—the data form or the data list—so choose the view you want before you print. Task 49 explains how to print in Works.

Displaying a Different Record in Form View

List view makes it easy to move to the record you want. You can simply scroll to it and click it. The data form (Form view) doesn't make moving around so obvious. You have to use buttons to the left of the horizontal scroll bar to move between records in the Form view.

Task 30: Moving Between Records in Form View

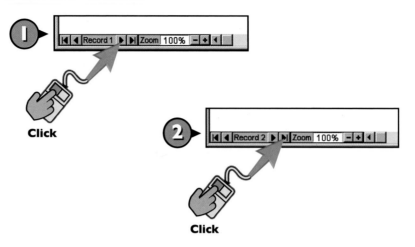

Click

Click

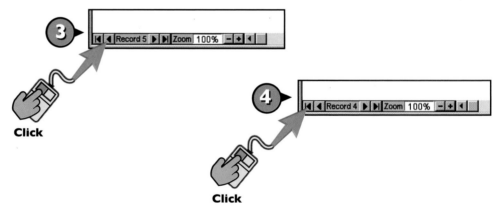

Click

Click

① ► Click the **next record** button to display the next record.

② ► Click the **last record** button to move to the end of the database, displaying a new, blank record.

③ ► Click the **previous record** button to display the previous record.

④ ► Click the **first record** button to display the very first record in the database.

Task 31: Using Go To to Jump to a Field

Start Here

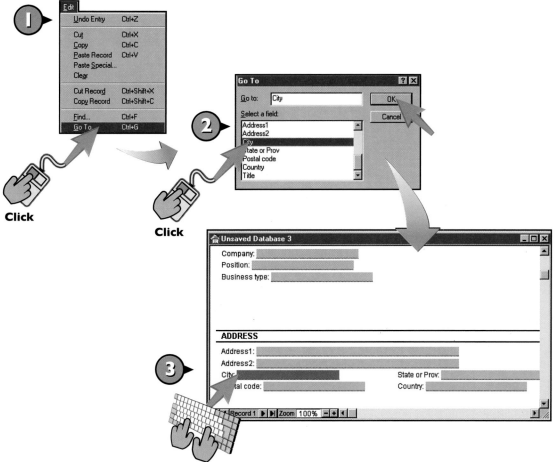

Click

Click

End Task

Going to a Specific Field

You can think of the Form view as displaying a "page" of information at a time. Trouble is, the page can be much larger than your computer screen, depending on the number of fields in the database. If your database has many fields and you want to jump between them in the Form view rather than scrolling to select a field, you can use the **Go To** command to get there.

✓ Going to a List View Field

You also can use the **Go To** command in List view. First, click in a field in the record you want to work with. Then use **Go To** to select the field you want in that record. However, the fastest way to select fields in the List view is to press the **Tab** key or click the field you want.

---

1 With the record you want to navigate displayed, choose **Edit**, **Go To**.

2 Click the field to go to in the **Select a Field** list and click **OK**.

3 Type a new field entry or view the entry in the selected field.

Task 32: Finding a Record

Using Find to Display a Record

If you have dozens or hundreds of records in your database, you don't have to sit and move through the records one by one to find a record you want. You can instead perform a find to display the record you need. You enter the information to match (from any field in the database) and then tell Works to display the next matching record or all matching records.

✓ **Controlling the Find's Starting Point**
You can perform a find in both the List view and the Form view. The Find operation starts from the currently displayed record, so if you want to be sure that Works examines all the records (if you find the next record instead of all of them), press **Ctrl+Home** to display the first record before performing the find.

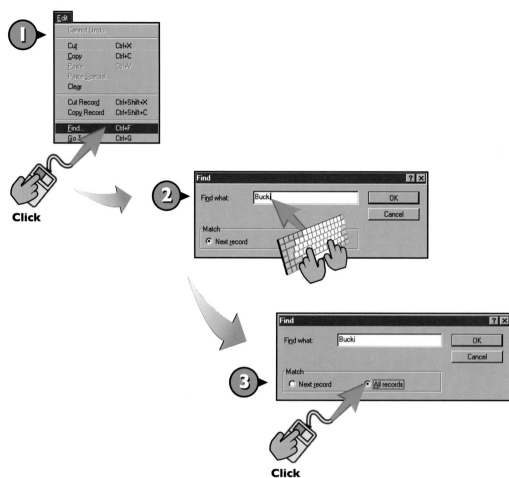

Start Here

Click

Click

1 Choose **Edit**, **Find** (Ctrl+F).

2 Type a field entry from the record(s) to find in the **Find What** text box.

3 If you want to find all the matching records rather than only the next match, click **All Records**, and then click **OK**.

Next Step

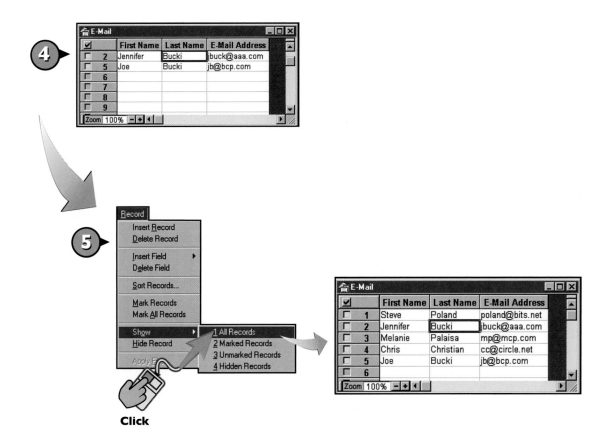

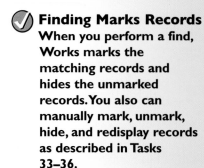

 4 You can review the matching record(s) in the view you want. (Use the navigation buttons to the left of the horizontal scroll bar in Form view.) Intervening records are hidden.

5 To redisplay all the database records, choose **Record**, **Show**, **All Records**.

Click

Finding Marks Records
When you perform a find, Works marks the matching records and hides the unmarked records. You also can manually mark, unmark, hide, and redisplay records as described in Tasks 33–36.

Finding Marks Records
When you perform a find, Works marks the matching records and hides the unmarked records. You also can manually mark, unmark, hide, and redisplay records as described in Tasks 33–36.

Manually Marking and Unmarking Records in Form View

Long databases can become unwieldy when you have to move through all the records to find one or more records. When you perform a find, all the found records need a common entry in one of the fields. If you want to display a list of records that don't necessarily match, you need to mark the records; then you can show only the marked or unmarked records in your database (see Task 35). This task explains how to mark (and unmark) records in Form view. The next task explains how to mark and unmark records in List view.

✓ Checking a Record's Marking

To tell if a record is marked in Form view, open the Record menu and see whether Mark Record is checked.

Task 33: Marking and Unmarking Records in Form View

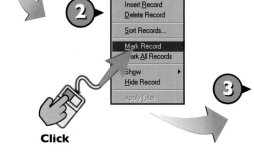

Click

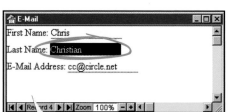

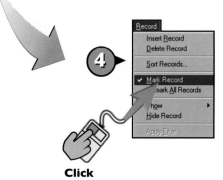

Click

1 Display a record to mark.

2 Choose **Record**, **Mark Record**. (Repeat steps 1 and 2 to mark additional records.)

3 Display a record to unmark.

4 Choose **Record**, **Mark Record** to clear the check beside that command. (Repeat steps 3 and 4 to unmark additional records.)

Task 34: Marking and Unmarking Records in List View

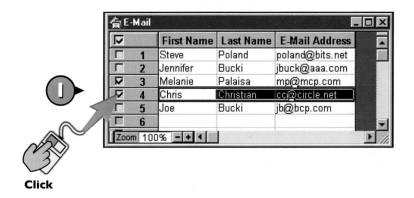

Click

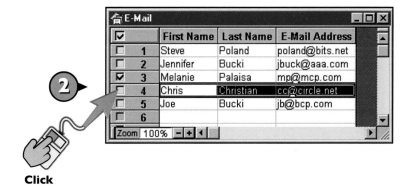

Click

 Click to place a check mark in the check box to the left of the record number for each record to mark.

 Click to clear the check mark in the check box to the left of the record number for each record to unmark.

Manually Marking and Unmarking Records in List View

In List view, marking and unmarking records resembles checking and clearing a check box.

 **Marking or Unmarking All Records**

You can mark or unmark all the records in the database by clicking the small check mark button in the upper-left corner of the database window. In Form view, choose **Record, Unmark All Records** to clear the marking.

Page
91

Displaying Marked or Unmarked Records

After you've marked the records you want, you can use that information to control which records appear in either the Form or List view. The steps are the same in either view, but this task shows the List view, where listing only selected records is more obvious.

✓ Hiding Records

Showing marked or unmarked records is different from hiding a record. Hiding a record means that it doesn't display at all (when you show marked, unmarked, or all records). To hide a record, display it in Form view or click a cell in it in List view. Choose **Record, Hide Record.** To redisplay the hidden records in the database, choose **Record, Show, Hidden Records.**

Task 35: Showing Only Marked and Unmarked Records

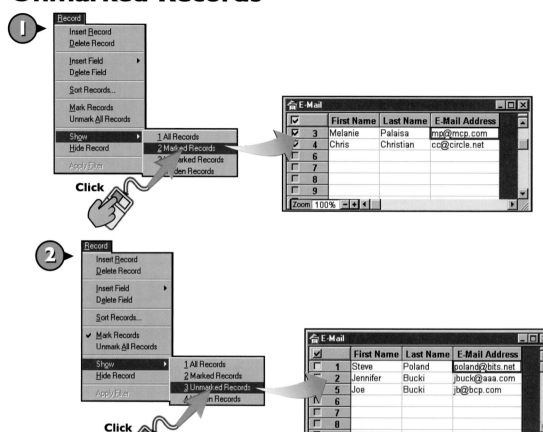

 Choose **Record**, **Show**, **Marked Records** to show only the marked records.

 Choose **Record**, **Show**, **Unmarked Records** to show only the unmarked records.

Task 36: Redisplaying All Records

Start Here

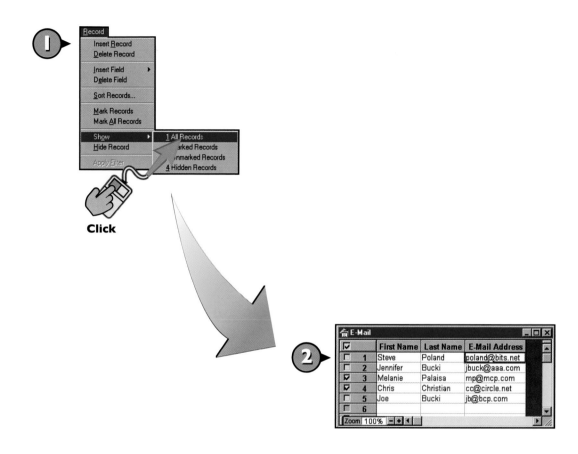

Click

Showing All the Records

When you want to see all the records in your database rather than just marked or unmarked records, you need to redisplay all the records in the database.

① Choose **Record**, **Show**, **All Records**.

② Resume working with the full database of records.

Showing Records Not Found
As noted in the last step of Task 32, "Finding a Record," after you perform a find, you also need to use the procedure described here to redisplay all the records in the database.

Task 37: Sorting Records

Changing the Order of Records

The database lists your records in the order in which you originally entered them, no matter what type of database you create. However, you can sort the data according to the entries in one or more fields. That is, if you want to reorder the records alphabetically according to last name, you can sort by the Last Name field. If you sort by more than one field, such as the Last Name field and then the First Name field, the database tool first sorts all records by Last Name. Then, if any records have the same entry in the Last Name field, the database tool sorts those records again according to the first name.

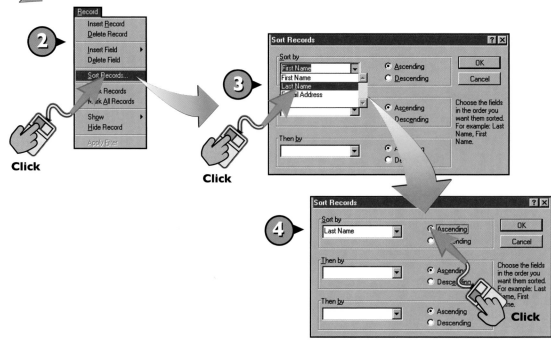

Click

Click

Click

1. Display the database to sort in the view that you want to work with.

2. Choose **Record**, **Sort Records**.

3. Choose the field to sort by first from the **Sort By** drop-down list.

4. Click **Ascending** or **Descending** to choose the sort order.

Next Step

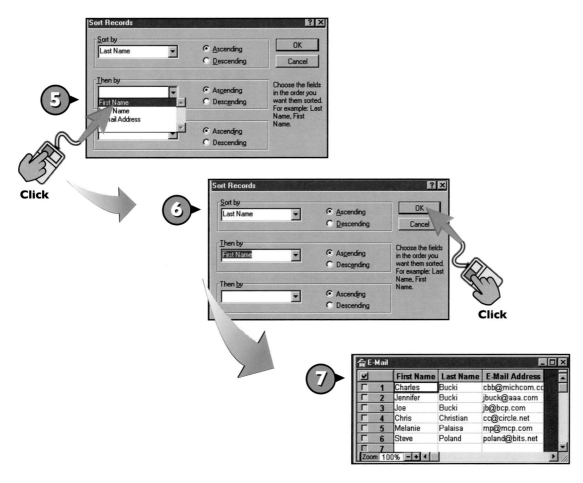

Click

Click

✓ Choosing a Sort Order
The ascending sort order sorts records in A–Z or 1, 2, 3 order. The descending sort order sorts records in Z–A or 3, 2, 1 order.

✓ Undoing a Sort
If you want to undo a sort, choose **Edit, Undo Sort** to do so before you save the file or perform another action. Otherwise, you won't be able to undo the sort. However, if you want to be able to return records to their original order, create a Record Number or ID field when you create the database, then enter the number for each record as you create it.

✓ Creating a Sorted Printout
Sort your database before you print if you want the records to appear in a particular order in the printout.

5 ▶ Use the two **Then By** drop-down lists to specify a second (and third) sort field and sort order, if needed.

6 ▶ Click **OK**.

7 ▶ View and work with the sorted records.

End Task

Task 38: Inserting a Record

Adding a Record in a Database

Databases tend to grow over time. Just as you need to add new entries in your paper address book, you may need to add new records into your database. You can add a new record at the end of the database in the Form view by pressing **Ctrl+End**, typing the new record information (press **Tab** between fields), and pressing **Tab** to finish the record. Or you can click the first blank row in the List view and enter new record information.

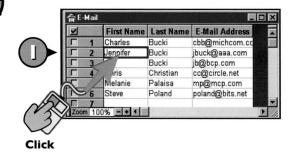

Click

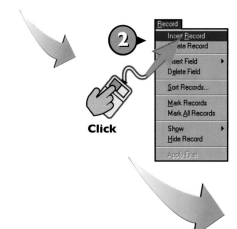

Click

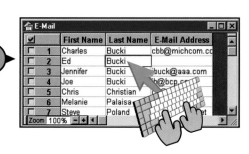

✓ Adding a New Field

You also can insert a new field in all of the records. It's easiest to do so in the List view. Right-click the field name beside which you want to add a new field, point to **Insert Field**, and click **Before or After**. Use the Insert Field dialog box to specify a **Field Name** and **Format**, click **Add**, and then click **Done**.

 Select the record before which you want to insert a new record. (Display the record in Form view or click a cell in it in List view.)

 Choose **Record**, **Insert Record**.

 Enter the field contents for the new record.

Task 39: Deleting a Record

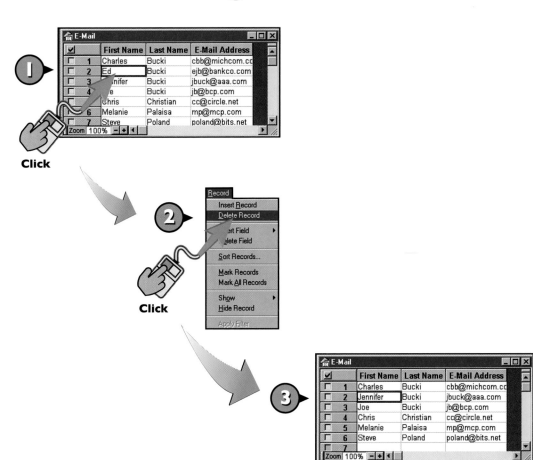

Click

Click

Removing a Database Record

What goes in can come out. You not only add records to update your database, but also delete records with obsolete or inaccurate information. You can delete a record in either the Form view or the List view.

ⓘ WARNING

Works does not warn you before it deletes a record. If you mistakenly delete a record, immediately choose **Edit, Undo Delete Record** to reinstate it. Also, I recommend saving your database before deleting any records.

✓ Selecting More than One Record

You can choose multiple contiguous records in List view, and then use the **Record, Delete Record** to delete all of them. To select multiple records, click the row (record) number for the first record to delete. Press and hold the **Shift** key, and click the row number for the last record to delete.

Select the record you want to delete. (Display the record in Form view or click a cell in it in List view.)

Choose **Record**, **Delete Record**.

You can work with the remaining database records.

Dialing the Modem with Easy Connect

If your computer system includes a modem, you're not limited to dialing in to the Internet (covered in Part 4). By using your modem and phone line, you can dial up a friend's computer to exchange files. Or you can dial a **BBS** (bulletin board service). You can connect to another computer or **BBS** using the Easy Connect feature in the Works communications tool.

✅ Getting Modem Setup Help

Tasks 40 through 47 assume your modem is correctly set up on your computer, including specifying a default location (under Windows). See the online Help that came with Windows if you need to learn more about setting up your modem.

Task 40: Using Easy Connect to Dial Another Computer

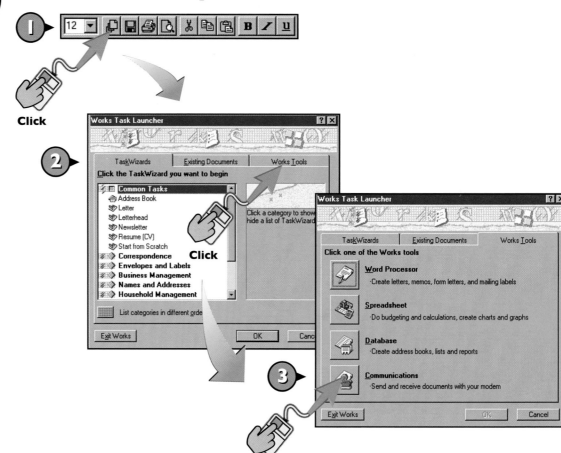

Click

Click

Click

Click

Click the **Task Launcher** button to redisplay the Task Launcher if needed.

Click the **Works Tools** tab.

Click the **Communications** button.

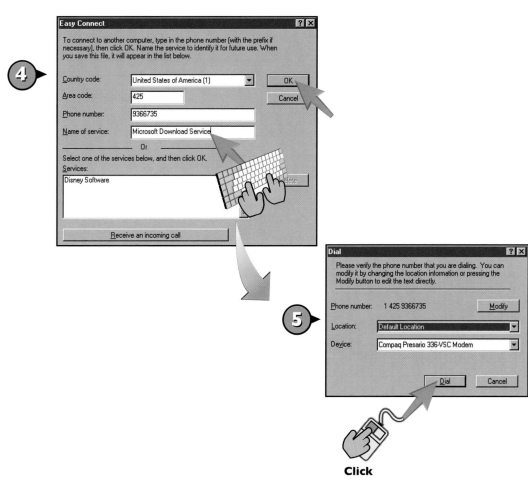

Click

④ Enter the **Area Code**, **Phone Number** to dial, and **Name of Service** (or your friend's name), and then click **OK**.

⑤ Verify the **Phone Number**, **Location** (that you're dialing from) and **Device** (lists the correct modem), and click **Dial** to dial the modem.

✓ Preparing to Dial

Before you dial another computer or BBS, make sure you have the phone number you need to dial. Also make sure you and your online partner have agreed on communications settings, or that you've identified the correct settings for the BBS you want to dial. Common choices are 8 data bits, None for Parity, and 1 for Stop Bits (this is 8-N-1 in shorthand).

✓ Dialing Again with Easy Connect

After it successfully dials and connects with the computer or BBS you specify, Easy Connect automatically saves the connection information you entered in a communications file. The next time you want to dial that BBS or user, choose **Phone, Easy Connect,** and double-click the desired connection in the **Services** list. Verify the settings and click **Dial**.

Task 41: Logging On if Needed

Logging On to a BBS

After the communications tool dials another computer, your next actions depend on what computer you dialed into. If you dialed up a friend's computer, each of you can begin typing messages to each other. Type a message and press **Enter** to send it.

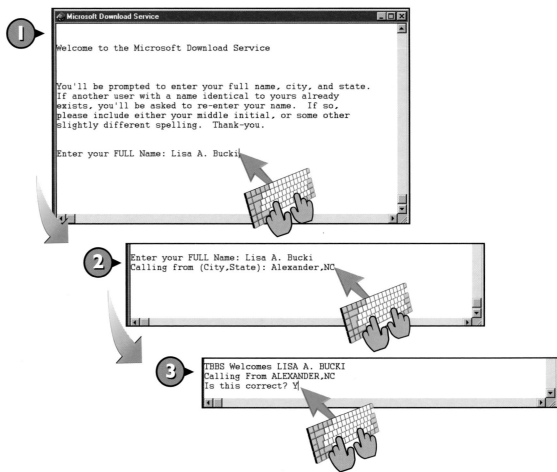

Start Here

Microsoft Download Service

```
Welcome to the Microsoft Download Service


You'll be prompted to enter your full name, city, and state.
If another user with a name identical to yours already
exists, you'll be asked to re-enter your name.  If so,
please include either your middle initial, or some other
slightly different spelling.  Thank-you.


Enter your FULL Name: Lisa A. Bucki
```

```
Enter your FULL Name: Lisa A. Bucki
Calling from (City,State): Alexander,NC
```

```
TBBS Welcomes LISA A. BUCKI
Calling From ALEXANDER,NC
Is this correct? Y
```

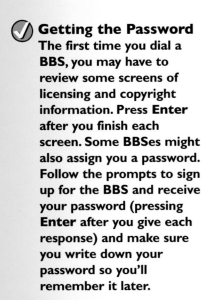

✓ **Getting the Password**
The first time you dial a BBS, you may have to review some screens of licensing and copyright information. Press **Enter** after you finish each screen. Some BBSes might also assign you a password. Follow the prompts to sign up for the BBS and receive your password (pressing **Enter** after you give each response) and make sure you write down your password so you'll remember it later.

1 Type your name when prompted, then press **Enter**.

2 If you're prompted to enter additional information such as a password or location, type it and press **Enter**.

3 Respond to any other prompts, pressing **Enter** after each response.

End Task

Task 42: Giving BBS Commands

Start Here

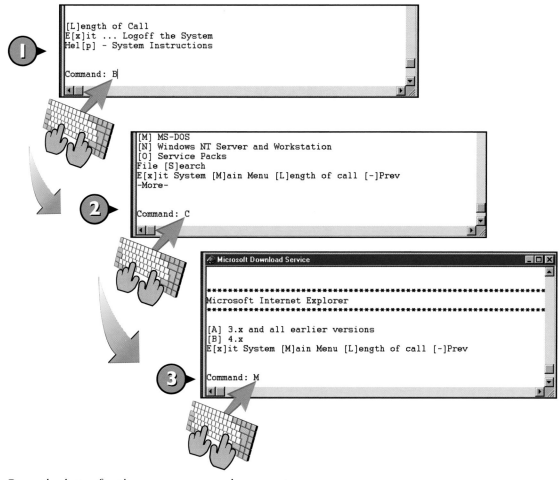

```
[L]ength of Call
E[x]it ... Logoff the System
Hel[p] - System Instructions


Command: B
```

```
[M] MS-DOS
[N] Windows NT Server and Workstation
[O] Service Packs
File [S]earch
E[x]it System [M]ain Menu [L]ength of call [-]Prev
-More-


Command: C
```

```
Microsoft Download Service                          _ □ X

**************************************************************
Microsoft Internet Explorer
**************************************************************

[A] 3.x and all earlier versions
[B] 4.x
E[x]it System [M]ain Menu [L]ength of call [-]Prev


Command: M
```

Using BBS Commands

For the most part, you'll need to interact with a **BBS** you dial into by using the keyboard. The **BBS** typically lists a menu of choices. Press the letter for the choice you want. This will either be the first letter of the command name or a letter that's highlighted or set off by brackets within the command name. You might be required to press **Enter** after you type the menu choice.

✓ **Learning About the BBS**
If you're new to the **BBS**, check out any help it offers. Most **BBSes** provide help about its menus and features.

✓ **Moving On in Your BBS**
Any time your **BBS** presents an information screen or a prompt such as "-More-," read the information and press **Enter** to continue.

① Press the letter for the menu command you want.

② Repeat to work your way through other menus.

③ Enter the command to return to the main BBS menu, usually **M** for menu or **S** for Stop.

End Task

Adjusting Your Communication Settings

If you connect to another computer and all you see is nonsense characters onscreen, your communication settings probably aren't working with the other computer's. Here's how to change them from 8-N-1 (the default) to 7-E-1.

Task 43: Changing Communication Settings

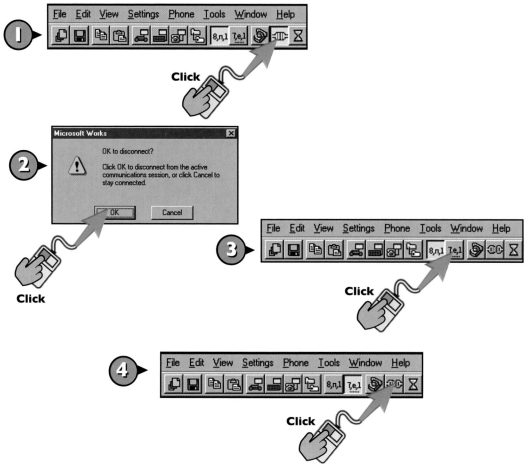

Click

Click

Click

Click

① ▶ Click the **Dial/Hangup** button or choose **Phone, Hang Up**.

② ▶ Click **OK** to finish disconnecting.

③ ▶ Click the **7-E-1 Settings** button to change your settings.

④ ▶ Click the **Dial/Hangup** button or choose **Phone, Dial Again** to dial the connection again.

End Task

Task 44: Changing the File Transfer Protocol

 Start Here

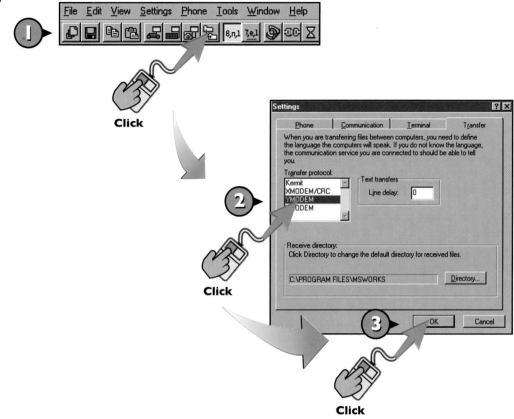

Click

Click

Click

Adjusting Your File Transfer Settings

In addition to using the correct communication settings, you need to choose the correct file transfer protocol (file transfer setting) to download any files from the **BBS** or computer you're connected to. The file transfer protocol is a communication method for sending files. Both computers must be using the same file transfer protocol.

✓ **What Downloading Is**
When you *download* a file, you transfer a copy of it (via modem) from the computer you're connected to and save it to your hard disk.

✓ **Choosing a Download Folder**
If you want to change the default folder where Works stores downloaded files, click the **Directory** button on the **Transfer** tab of the Settings dialog box, use the **Directories** and **Drives** lists to select another folder, and click **OK**. You can ignore the Line Delay setting on the Transfer tab.

---

1 ▶ Click the **Transfer Settings** button or choose **Settings**, **Transfer**.

2 ▶ Click the setting to use in the **Transfer Protocol** list.

3 ▶ Click the **OK** button.

 End Task

Task 45: Downloading a File to Your Computer

Making a File Transfer

Many users go online to find files to download. BBSes and a number of online services offer a wealth of free software (freeware), software patches (fixes for previously released programs), and free documents. In addition, you can download *shareware*, programs distributed on the honor system; you can download and distribute a shareware program for free, but if you plan to use it regularly, you should send the requested fee to the shareware author.

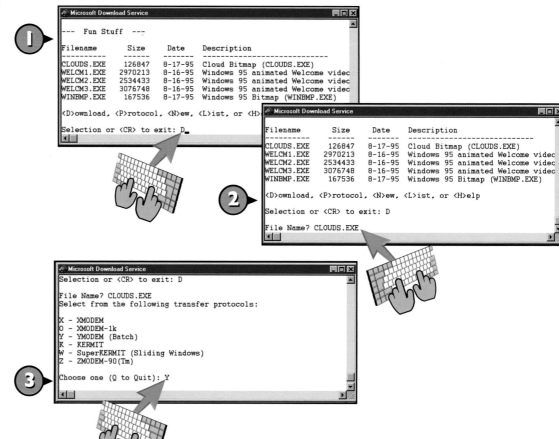

> **WARNING**
> The downloading process may vary slightly from BBS to BBS. For example, the BBS may prompt you to enter a protocol and file name and storage location for the downloaded file.

① Press **D** for download (or give the corresponding command required by your BBS) and press **Enter** if needed.

② If prompted, type the name or menu number for the file to download and press **Enter**.

③ When prompted, specify the transfer protocol to use, and then press **Enter** if needed.

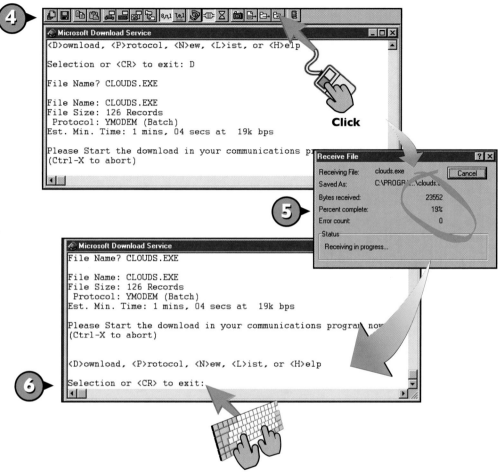

Trying Uppercase
Some BBSes require you to enter commands, filenames, and other selections in all uppercase characters and some don't. (I've used uppercase just to make the screens here easier to read.) If a BBS won't respond to your command, try typing it in uppercase or with the exact capitalization shown onscreen.

Choosing a Protocol
If the BBS offers a protocol choice as shown in step 1, you can use that command to verify or choose a file transfer protocol.

Naming Your File
If you're prompted to enter a filename, try to give your downloaded files the same name that the BBS uses.

4 ▶ When prompted, click the **Receive Binary File** button or choose **Tools**, **Receive File**.

5 ▶ Monitor the transfer progress. This dialog box closes when the transfer finishes.

6 ▶ Press **Enter** to continue working after the download finishes.

Task 46: Logging Off and Hanging Up

Finishing Your BBS Connection

After you finish downloading files and viewing the information available on a BBS, you should log off from the BBS and hang up your modem connection. BBS uses a variety of different logoff commands, including Quit, Goodbye, Logoff, Bye, and Exit.

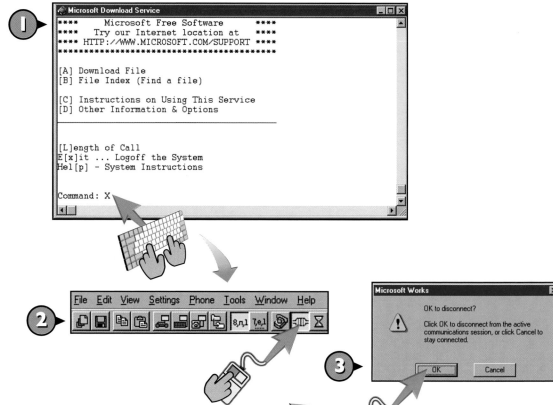

Click

Click

⚠ WARNING

Although it's rare, you may have problems logging back in to a BBS or online service if you don't log off correctly. Always log off, unless you're having some type of problem communicating with the BBS.

① Type the logoff command for your BBS and press **Enter** if needed.

② If the communications tool doesn't hang up automatically, click the **Dial/Hangup** button.

③ Click **OK** if prompted to verify that you want to disconnect.

Task 47: Exiting the Communications Tool

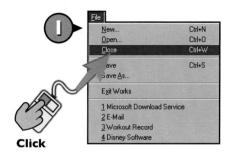

Click

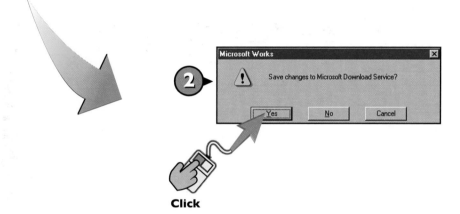

Click

Shutting Down the Communications Tool

You can exit the communications tool without exiting Works by closing the open communication window (file). Actually, this technique works in the other Works tools, too!

1 Choose **File**, **Close**.

2 Click **Yes** to save your changes to the communications tool file and close the communications tool.

Displaying Another Works File or Tool

You can create or open as many Works files as you want during a single sitting at your computer. Only one file can be active (or current, or selected) at a time, and the current file determines which Works tool's menus and toolbar buttons appear. To switch to another Works tool, you either have to create a new file using the desired Works tool or display another file created in a different Works tool, as described in this task.

Task 48: Switching Between Open Files (and Tools)

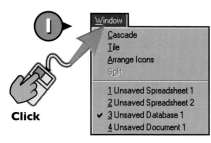

Start Here

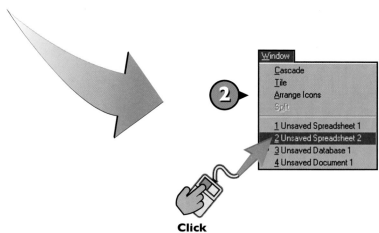

Click

Click

Reopening a File
Use the **File, Open** command to open a Works file that you've previously saved as described in Task 50.

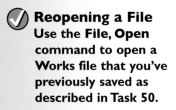

① Open the **Window** menu.

② Click the name of the file to switch tool to immediately display the file and the applicable Works tool.

End Task

Task 49: Printing a File

Start Here

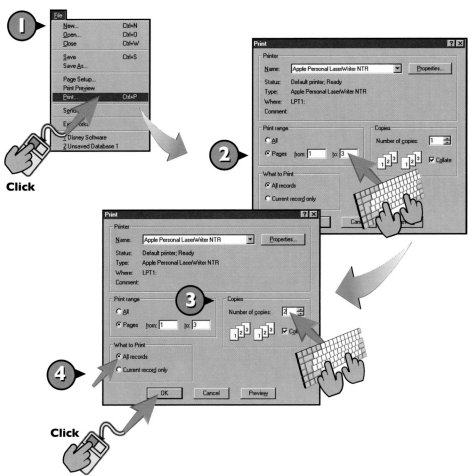

Click

Click

Making a Printout in Works

No matter which Works tool you're presently using, the process for printing the current file is the same. You can print all the pages in the file or specify a range of pages using the **From** and **To** text boxes. You also can enter a number of copies to print. The only differences appear in what or how you can print. For a word processor file, you can print the main document or an envelope (if you've created one). For a spreadsheet, you can choose draft quality printing to print a draft. For a database, you can print all records or the current record only.

① Choose **File**, **Print**.

② To print only a range of pages, click **Pages** and enter the number of the first and last page to print in the **From** and **To** text boxes.

③ To print multiple copies, change the **Number of Copies** text box entry.

④ Change any other settings and click **OK** to print.

✓ **Printing in a Snap**
To print one copy of the current Works file with the default printing settings, click the **Print** button on the toolbar.

End Task

Task 50: Saving and Closing a File

Saving and Closing in Works

As in Word 97, saving a file in a Works tool stores the file to disk so that you can work with it later. After you save a particular file, you can close it so that you can concentrate on working with another Works tool.

Click

Click

✓ **Saving Reminder**
If you forget to save a file or your changes to it and try to exit Works or close the file, Works reminds you to save the file.

 Click the **Save** button on the toolbar.

 To save to a disk or folder other than the default one, open the **Save In** list and select the folder to use.

 Click in the **File Name** text box and enter the filename to use.

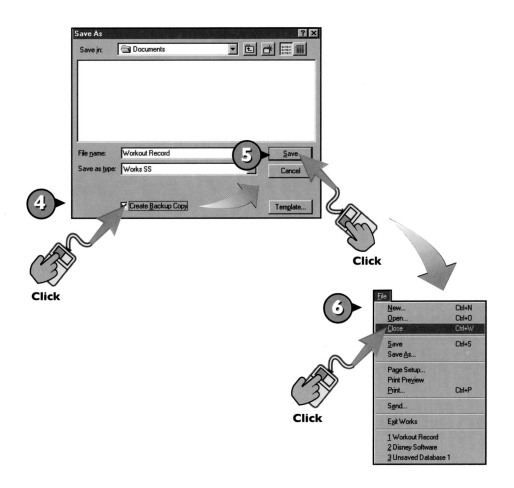

Click

Click

Click

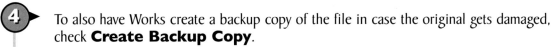

(4) To also have Works create a backup copy of the file in case the original gets damaged, check **Create Backup Copy**.

(5) Click the **Save** button.

(6) Choose **File**, **Close** to close the file after you've saved it.

✓ **Saving for Safety**
After you save your file the first time, you should save it every 10 minutes or so thereafter by clicking the Save button.

✓ **Using Your Backup File**
If you accidentally delete your original file or it somehow becomes damaged so that you can't open it, you can open the backup file if you've created one. To do so, choose **File**, **Open**. Choose **Backup Files (*.b*)** from the **Files of Type** drop-down list. Use the **Look In** list if needed to select the disk and folder holding the backup file, click the file when it appears in the dialog box, and click **Open**.

End Task

Tracking Your Finances with Money 98

You can use your home computer to get yourself organized once and for all. One important area of your life that you can organize with a computer is your finances. This part shows you how to use Microsoft Money 98 to set up a checking account, enter bills and other transactions, print checks, set up a budget, and track investments.

Tasks

Task 1: Starting and Exiting Money

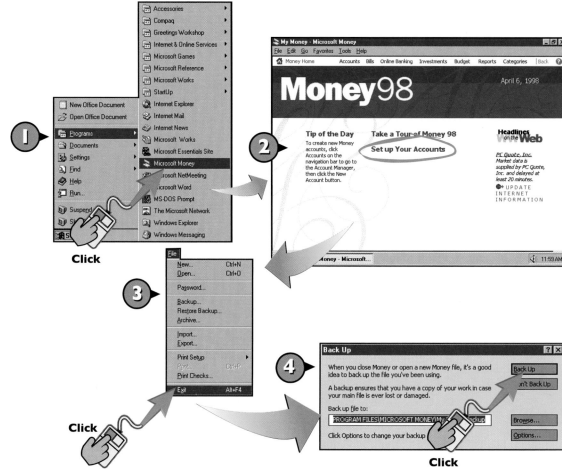

Starting and Closing the Money Program

Financial organizer (or *financial management*) *software* tracks money you add to and remove from your bank account (or another type of account, such as an investment account), and lets you enter and print checks and create a budget. Microsoft Home Essentials includes the Money 98 financial organizer software. You can use Money to organize and update your financial information.

✓ Touring Money

The first time you start Money 98, it tells you that it's creating and opening a new file. Then, the Microsoft Money – Tour dialog box appears. If you want to view an onscreen tour of the money program, insert the Home Essentials Disc 1 CD-ROM in your CD-ROM drive and click Retry. Otherwise, click Cancel to close the dialog box and start working with Money 98.

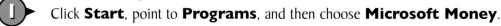

1 ▶ Click **Start**, point to **Programs**, and then choose **Microsoft Money**.

2 ▶ When the Money Home screen opens, you can set up your accounts or otherwise work in Money.

3 ▶ Choose **File**, **Exit** or press **Alt+F4** when you're ready to exit Money.

4 ▶ Click **Back Up** in the Back Up dialog box to create a back up copy of your file before the program closes.

Task 2: Creating a Money File

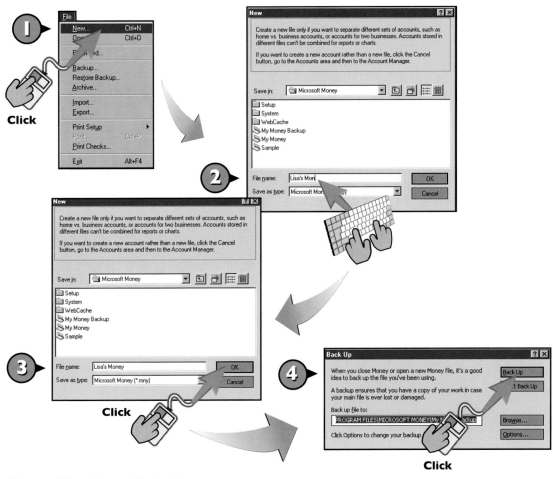

Click

Click

Click

Creating a File for Your Financial Information

Money stores the different types of financial information you enter in a file. The first time you start the Money program, it automatically creates the first file for you and names the file *My Money*. If you'll be the only one in your household using Money, you can start using the My Money file. If more than one person will be using Money and each person's financial information needs to stay separated, then each user needs to create and name his or her own Money file.

✓ **Choosing a Money File**
When you start Money, it opens the file you most recently used (or created). To work with the financial information in a different Money file, you need to open the Money file you want to use. See Task 18 to learn how to open the file of your choice.

---

1 ▶ Choose **File**, **New** (Ctrl+N).

2 ▶ Type the name for the new file in the File Name text box.

3 ▶ Click **OK**.

4 ▶ Click **Back Up** to create a backup copy of the previously opened file, close the old file, and create and open the new file.

Task 3: Setting Up a Checking Account

Creating Your Checking Account

Within each Money file, you create *accounts* to track your savings, checking, and investment accounts. You enter information about each transaction you perform with that account's funds into the account in Money. When you create a checking account in Money, you can enter a bill *transaction* into that checking account and then print a hard copy (paper) check to pay each bill.

✅ Displaying the Account Manager
You also can display the Account Manager screen by choosing **Go, Accounts** (Ctrl+Shift+A). If you don't see icons for various accounts and buttons for managing accounts but instead see a register for an existing account, click the **Account Manager** button to the right of the account name.

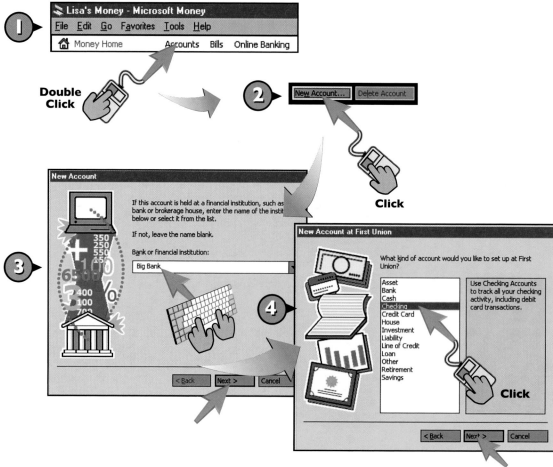

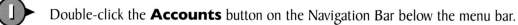

1. Double-click the **Accounts** button on the Navigation Bar below the menu bar.

2. Click the **New Account** button at the bottom of the Account Manager screen.

3. Enter the name of your bank in the Bank or Financial Institution text box and then click **Next**.

4. Leave **Checking** selected in the next dialog box, then click **Next**. Edit the suggested account name, if needed, and click **Next**.

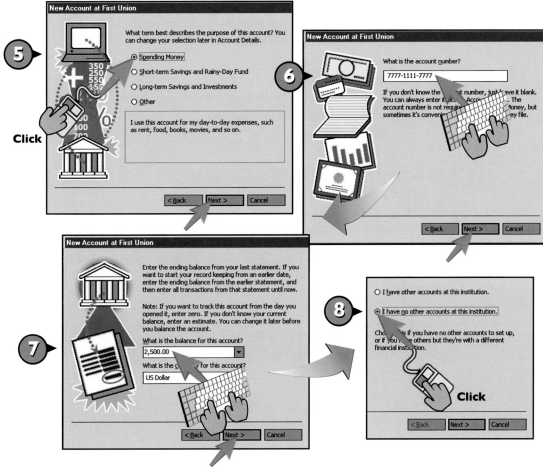

Creating a Savings Account

Setting up a savings account is nearly identical to the process described here. Just select a savings account instead of a checking account. An investment account is a bit different, though. Task 15 explains how to set up an account to track your mutual fund or stock investments.

WARNING

You need to be sure to synchronize the checking account balance you enter in Money when you create the account with the balance of your real account with your bank. To do so, work from your most recent, balanced checking account statement from your bank.

5 ▶ Click the option button that best describes the account's purpose (usually Spending Money for checking) and click **Next**.

6 ▶ Enter the account number and click **Next**.

7 ▶ Enter the account balance and click **Next**.

8 ▶ At the next dialog box, leave **I Have No Other Accounts at This Institution** selected and click **Next**, **Finish**.

Making Categories to Identify Income and Expenses

To master your budget, you need to understand where your money comes from and where it goes. In Money 98, you assign a *category* and *subcategory* to each transaction to identify how you made or spent the money involved. You can then use Money to generate reports totaling money you made (or spent) in each category or subcategory. Money offers predefined categories and subcategories. For example, it offers a Household category, which contains a Furnishings subcategory. You can add your own category or subcategory to supplement the list, such as if you want a Cleaning subcategory for the Household category.

Task 4: Creating Categories and Subcategories

Start Here

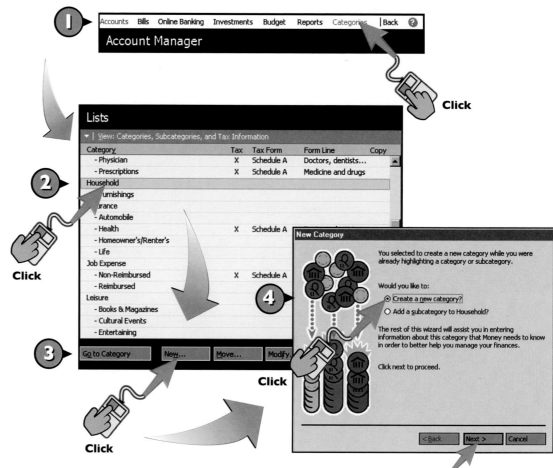

Click

1 ▶ Click the **Categories** button on the navigation bar below the menu bar.

2 ▶ To create a new subcategory, click a category in the Lists list. Otherwise, don't click anything.

3 ▶ Click the **New** button at the bottom of the Categories & Payees screen.

4 ▶ Select **Create a New Category?** or **Add a Subcategory to (*Category*)** to create either a category or subcategory. Click **Next**.

Next Step

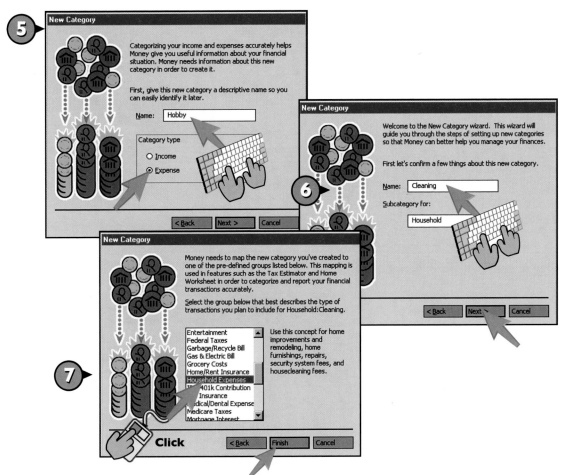

5 For a new category, enter a **Name**, then choose either the **Income** or **Expense** option button.

6 For a subcategory, enter the **Name**. Click **Next**.

7 Click the concept to assign to the category in the list of concepts, then click **Finish**.

✅ **Creating a Report**
To display a report after you've entered some transactions, click the **Reports** button on the navigation bar and click a report category in the list at the left side of the screen. Then click the report you want in the Gallery of Reports and Charts and click the **Go to Report/Chart** button at the bottom of the screen.

✅ **Getting the Concept**
Concepts group categories and subcategories provide further reporting effectiveness in Money. For example, you might want to assign the Household Expenses concept to the Food category, the Bills category, and the Household category.

Task 5: Viewing Accounts and Opening an Account

Accessing Account Information

Even if you've created only one account and added a few categories using the steps in this part, you've already used the navigation bar to display different Money 98 features. At any point, when you're ready to enter transactions into or otherwise work with an account, you need to use the navigation bar to return to the Account Manager.

✓ **Understanding Transaction Forms**

You enter checks, deposits, transfers, withdrawals, and cash machine (ATM) transactions in the transaction forms, which look like a series of tabs at the bottom of the transaction register. If you don't see the transaction forms when you display the register, click the **View** drop-down list arrow below the account name and click **Transaction Forms** in the menu that appears.

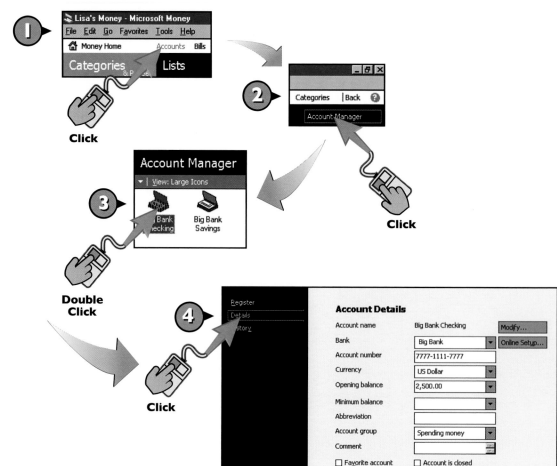

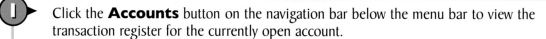

① Click the **Accounts** button on the navigation bar below the menu bar to view the transaction register for the currently open account.

② To display the accounts in the current Money file, click the **Account Manager** button near the upper-right corner of the screen.

③ To view the transaction register for the account you want to use, double-click the account's icon.

④ Click **Details**, then change any information about the account, as needed, in the text boxes of the Account Details screen.

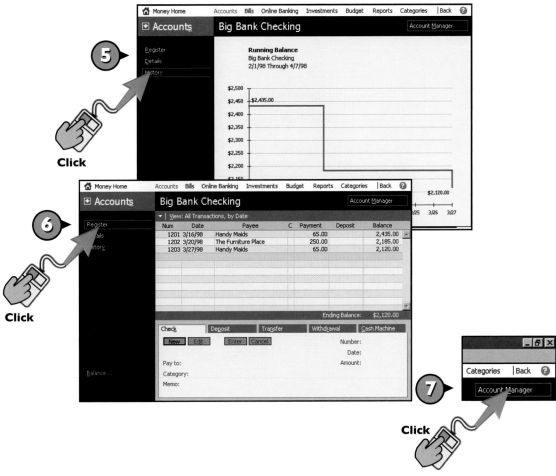

WARNING
Changing the Bank text box entry on the Account Details screen doesn't change the account name. To change the Account Name, click the **Modify** button on the Account Details screen. In the Modify Account dialog box that appears, enter a new account name in the New Name text box. You also can change the account type by choosing an option button in the Account Type area of the dialog box. However, changing account types can really mess up data transactions you've previously entered; for example, if you've entered bills (checks) in a bank account, you don't want to change it to a credit card account. After you finish making your changes in the Modify Account dialog box, click **OK** to close it.

Click **History** to view a running balance of account expenditures.

Click **Register** to redisplay the transaction register.

Click the **Account Manager** button to redisplay the Account Manager screen so you can open another account.

Task 6: Entering a Bill (Check)

Writing a Check in Money

Once or twice a month, you sit down with your checkbook and bills, write out checks (bill payments) longhand, and write a corresponding transaction in your paper checkbook register. When you enter a check (bill) in Money and then use Money to print the check, you only have to enter the transaction once. Money records the check in the account register and correctly calculates the new account balance before you print the check.

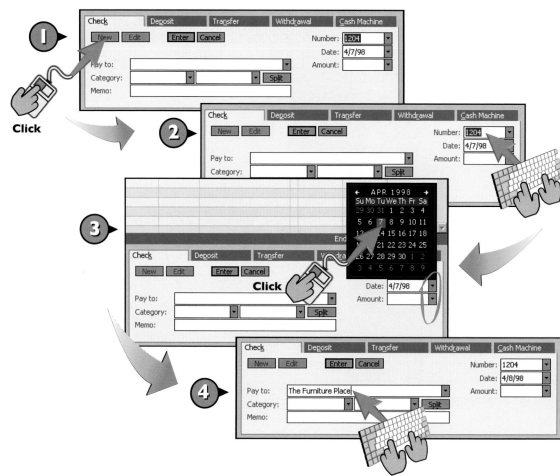

Start Here

Click

Click

✓ **Getting the Numbers Right**

When you enter a check (bill) in the checking account register, make sure you enter the correct check number. By default, Money numbers the first check #1001.

1. In the register for the checking account you want to use, click the **Check** transaction form tab.

2. Edit the check number in the **Number** text box, if needed, and press **Tab**.

3. Click the drop-down list arrow beside the **Date** text box, click the date for the check in the calendar that appears, and press **Tab**.

4. Enter a payee in the **Pay To** text box and press **Tab**.

Next Step

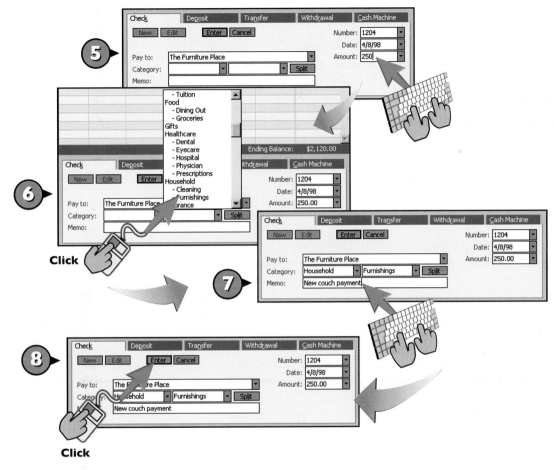

Click

Click

✓ **Postdating Checks**
You can postdate checks to any date that you would like.

✓ **Finding Out How to Print**
To learn to print checks from Money, see Task 11.

✓ **Remembering Payees**
After you enter a payee the first time, Money stores the payee name and transaction information in its payees list. Then, when you type the first few characters of the payee name in the Pay To text box, the rest of the name appears, and you can press Tab. You can then simply edit the Amount, Category, and Memo entries as needed.

✓ **Writing Another Check**
After you enter the first check, click the **New** button on the Check tab to begin entering the next check.

5 ▶ Enter the check amount in the **Amount** text box.

6 ▶ Choose a subcategory from the right **Category** drop-down list to assign a category and subcategory. (Using the left drop-down list assigns a category only.)

7 ▶ Press **Tab** twice, then enter a description or note in the **Memo** text box.

8 ▶ Click the **Enter** button on the Check tab to add the check to the register.

Task 7: Entering a Deposit

Adding a Deposit Transaction

After you write a few checks, you may have depleted quite a bit of money from your checking account. At some point, you'll need to deposit money into your checking account at your bank and record that transaction in your checking account in Money. Similarly, if you receive an electronic payment, such as an automatic payroll deposit or interest payment, you need to enter the deposit in your Money checking account. Money calculates the new balance, so you'll know how much you have available for further checks.

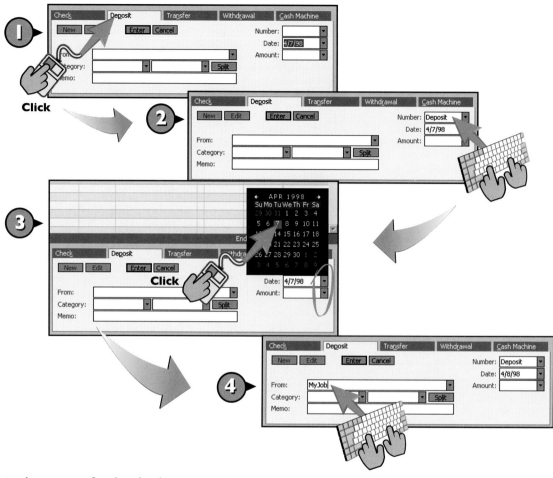

Click

Click

✓ Entering Similar Transactions

The steps described here for making a deposit into a checking account also work for a savings or cash account you've created in Money.

In the register for the checking account you want to use, click the **Deposit** transaction form tab.

Edit a notation such as **Deposit** in the Number text box, if needed. Press **Tab**.

Click the **Date** drop-down list arrow, click the date you made the deposit or the expected electronic deposit date, then press **Tab**.

Enter a payer in the **From** text box, then press **Tab**.

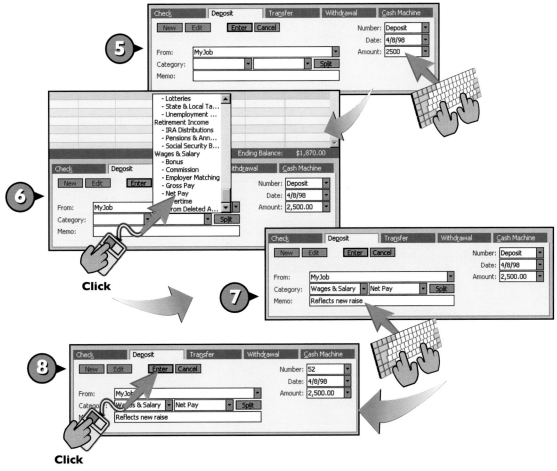

WARNING
The bank doesn't necessarily add the deposit amount to your balance until the deposit clears, which can take two to three days. So consider post-dating your deposits by two days or so, just to remind yourself that you may need to hold off check writing.

WARNING
Resist the temptation to wait until you receive your monthly statement to enter deposits and instead enter them when you make them. Money *will* let you overdraft your checking account so that it shows a negative balance. So, if you haven't entered your deposits, you'll have to remember how much you deposited and not exceed that amount when you write checks. This makes you vulnerable to real overdrafts if you make a mistake. Entering the deposits as you make them prevents such a situation.

5 ► Enter the deposit amount in the **Amount** text box.

6 ► Choose a subcategory from the **Category** drop-down list to assign a category and subcategory. (Using the left drop-down list assigns a category only.)

7 ► Press **Tab** twice, then enter a description or note in the **Memo** text box.

8 ► Click the **Enter** button on the Deposit tab to add the deposit to the register.

Transferring Money between Accounts

At many banks, you earn more interest in a savings account than a checking account. To maximize your interest returns you should keep as much money in savings and as little in checking as possible. This likely means you'll need to transfer money between the accounts, such as transferring part of a paycheck deposited into your checking account to your savings account. As with other transaction types, after you make the real transaction at your bank, you need to enter the transfer in your Money file. Money then calculates the new account balances.

✓ **Keeping It Simple**
Although you could enter a transfer as two separate transactions—a withdrawal from one account and a deposit into another—you can accomplish the feat faster by entering a single transfer transaction.

Task 8: Entering a Transfer

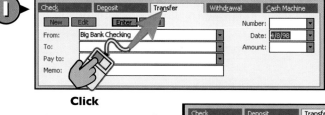

Click

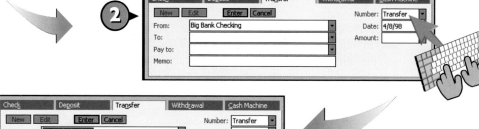

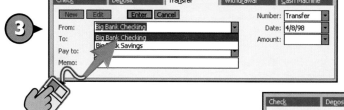

Click

Click

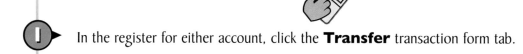

1 In the register for either account, click the **Transfer** transaction form tab.

2 Edit a notation such as **Transfer** in the Number text box, if needed. Press **Tab**.

3 Open the **From** drop-down list, then click the account out of which you want to transfer funds, if that account isn't already named.

4 Click the **To** drop-down list arrow, then click the account into which you want to transfer funds.

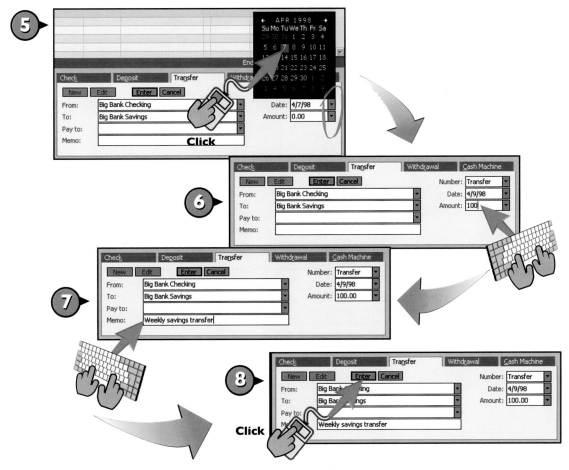

5 Click the **Date** drop-down list arrow, click the date you made the transfer, then press **Tab** twice.

6 Enter the transfer amount in the **Amount** text box.

7 Press **Tab** twice and enter a description or note in the **Memo** text box.

8 Click the **Enter** button on the Transfer tab to enter a transaction in the register for each of the accounts.

✔️ **Redisplaying the Transaction Forms**
Remember, if you don't see the transaction forms when you display the account register, click the **View** drop-down list arrow below the account name, then click **Transaction Forms** in the menu that appears.

✔️ **Editing a Transaction**
To edit any transaction, double-click it in the register. Make the changes you want in the text boxes on the selected transaction form tab at the bottom of the register, then click the **Enter** button to accept the changes.

End Task

Task 9: Entering a Withdrawal

Recording a Withdrawal

When you withdraw money from your bank using a withdrawal slip (rather than a check or **ATM** machine), you should enter that transaction as a withdrawal in your checking account (or savings account). When you enter the withdrawal, you can assign a category and subcategory to identify how you spent the money, or even a specific payee, if applicable.

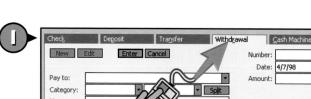

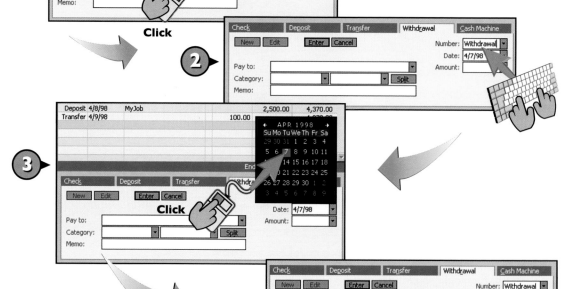

Click

Click

✓ Entering ATM Withdrawals

When you use an ATM to withdraw cash, enter the transaction on the Cash Machine transaction form tab rather than the Withdrawal transaction form tab.

1 ▶ In the register for the account, click the **Withdrawal** transaction form tab.

2 ▶ Edit a notation such as **Withdrawal** in the Number text box, if needed. Press **Tab**.

3 ▶ Click the **Date** drop-down list arrow, click the date you made the withdrawal, and press **Tab**.

4 ▶ Enter a payee, if needed, in the **Pay To** text box and press **Tab**.

Next Step ▶

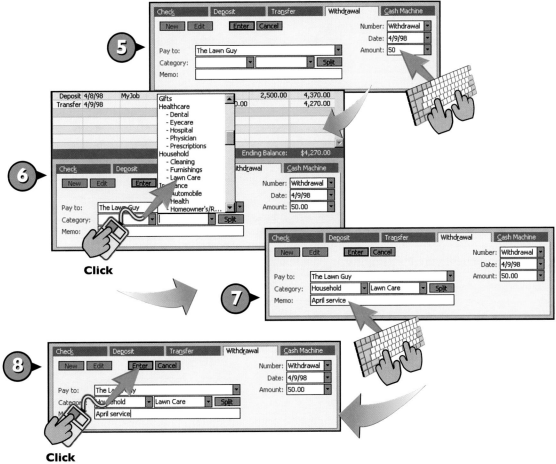

Click

Click

5 Enter the withdrawal amount in the **Amount** text box.

6 Choose a subcategory from the right **Category** drop-down list to assign a category and subcategory. (Using the left drop-down list assigns a category only.)

7 Press **Tab** twice, then enter a description or note in the **Memo** text box.

8 Click the **Enter** button on the Withdrawal tab to enter the transaction in the account register.

✓ **Editing a Transaction**
To edit any transaction, double-click it in the register. Make the changes you want in the text boxes on the selected transaction form tab at the bottom of the register, then click the **Enter** button to accept the changes.

✓ **Recording Bank Fees**
You can enter any extra bank fees charged to your account, such as stop payment fees, as withdrawals.

End Task

Entering Your ATM Transactions

ATM machines make it easy to get cash from your bank account at any hour. After you make an ATM withdrawal, you should record the transaction in your account in Money 98 using the Cash Machine tab of the register.

Task 10: Entering a Cash Machine Transaction

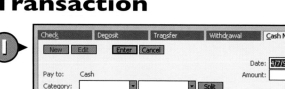

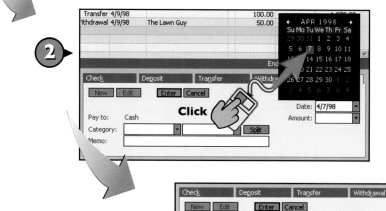

Click

Click

> ⓘ **WARNING**
> If you withdraw cash from an ATM machine that charges you a fee, don't forget to check your statement for fee amounts and enter those fees as withdrawals.

① In the register for the account, click the **Cash Machine** transaction form tab.

② Click the **Date** drop-down list arrow, click the date you made the withdrawal, and then press **Tab**.

③ Enter the ATM withdrawal amount in the **Amount** text box.

Next Step

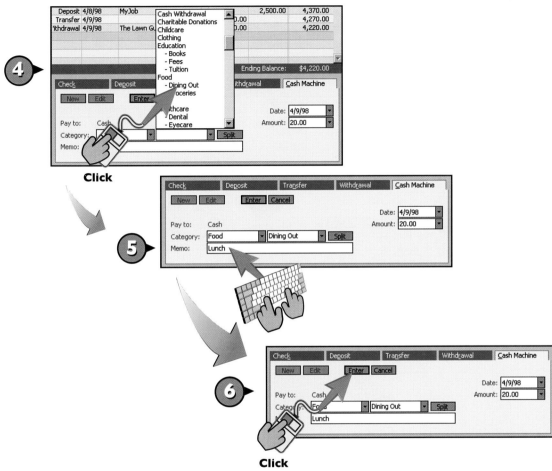

Click

Click

Click

4. Choose a subcategory from the right **Category** drop-down list to assign a category and subcategory. (Using the left drop-down list assigns a category only.)

5. Press **Tab** twice, then enter a description or note in the **Memo** text box.

6. Click the **Enter** button on the Cash Machine tab to enter the transaction in the account register.

✓ Tracking ATM Transactions

Jot down the purpose of each ATM withdrawal you make on the receipt from the ATM machine. That way, you'll be able to enter categories and subcategories for more ATM transactions. Then, Money will have a more accurate record of what you're spending money on.

End Task

Task 11: Printing Checks

Having Money Print Your Checks

While you probably won't cart your computer and printer with you so you can print checks while shopping, you may very well want to use Money 98 to print checks to pay bills. Printing checks saves you the trouble of handwriting them.

✔ **Editing a Check Transaction**

To edit a check, double-click the check transaction in the checking account register. In the Check transaction form tab, make the changes you want, then click the **Enter** button.

⚠ **WARNING**

Money sequentially numbers the transactions (changes the Number text box entry) when you print more than one check. So, if the checks you want to print should not be sequentially numbered in the register (say you want to print checks 1203 and 1205, but want to print 1204 at a later time), print the checks one at a time.

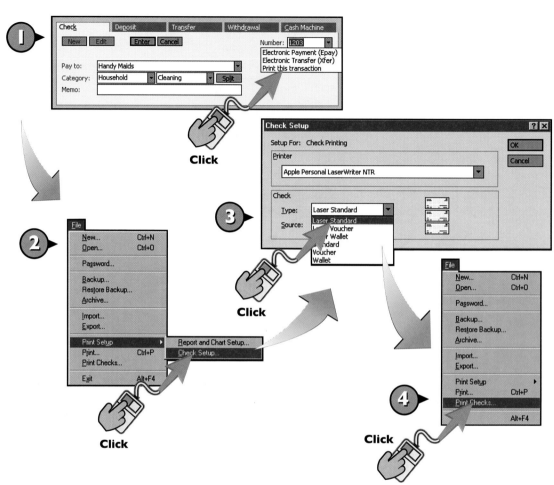

① For each check to print, select **Print This Transaction** from the Number drop-down list while entering or editing the check.

② Choose **File**, **Print Setup**, **Check Setup**.

③ Verify that the correct printer is selected, choose a check format from the Type drop-down list, then click **OK**.

④ Choose **File**, **Print Checks**.

Next Step ▶

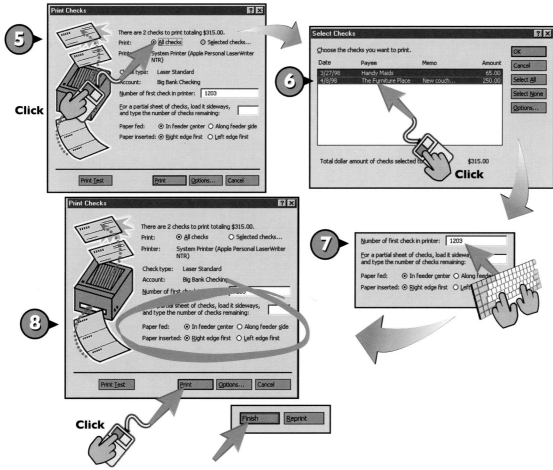

Click

Click

Click

WARNING

To print your checks from Money 98, you have to order special checks that work with your printer and have your account and bank information on them. Choose the **Help, Ordering Checks** command in Money to learn how to order checks. Then, load the checks into your printer before you begin the print process.

Checking Your Options

Depending on what printer and check format you've selected, different options appear below the **Number of First Check in Printer** text box of the **Print Checks** dialog box. Change the settings here depending on how many checks you're inserting into the printer, and so forth. To test your settings, insert a blank page into the printer, click **Print Test**, and then compare the results with your check format.

5. To print all checks, leave **All Checks** selected and go to step 7. To print only selected checks, click **Selected Checks**.

6. Click each check that you do not want to print to remove the highlighting, then click **OK**.

7. If needed, edit the entry in the **Number of First Check In Printer** text box to match the first check you've placed in the printer.

8. Review and correct the other options as needed, then click **Print**. Make sure your checks printed correctly, then click **Finish**.

End Task

Reconciling Your Checking Transactions

Just as you have to synchronize your bank records and paper checking account register, you have to synchronize your bank records and your Money 98 checking account register. This process is called reconciling, or balancing, your checkbook (checking account). As soon as possible after you get your monthly statement from the bank, you should use it to follow the reconciliation process described here, to keep your Money 98 account information as accurate as possible.

✓ **Reconciling Other Accounts**

You use the same basic steps as those described here to reconcile accounts other than checking accounts.

Task 12: Reconciling the Checking Account

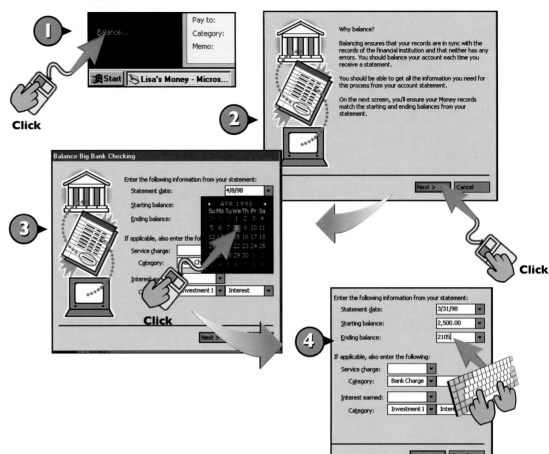

 With the checking account to reconcile open onscreen, click the **Balance** choice in the lower-left corner.

 Click **Next** in the Balance (Account) dialog box that appears.

 Specify the statement date using the Statement Date drop-down list.

 Verify that the Starting Balance matches the statement starting balance. Enter the statement ending balance in the Ending Balance text box.

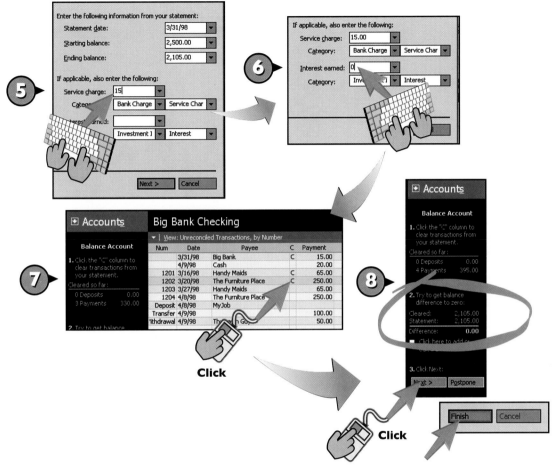

WARNING

Although you could use the Service Charge text box and Category drop-down list to enter a fee charged for a cash machine (ATM) transaction, this works only if you have one such fee (or take the time to manually total those fees). It also precludes you from entering the account service charge as you balance the account. It's a better bet to enter each cash machine transaction fee as a separate transaction in the register before you begin balancing the account. You can assign the Bank Charges or Cash Withdrawal category to each of these transactions, so Money 98 properly identifies these expenses.

Correcting Reconciliation Errors

If you fail to properly clear all your transactions and click Next, a dialog box appears to inform you that the account hasn't balanced and that there may be an error.

5 Enter any service charge listed on the statement in the **Service Charge** text box. Optionally, choose a subcategory from the right **Category** drop-down list.

6 Enter any interest listed on the statement in the **Interest** text box, then click **Next**.

7 To clear each transaction that appears on the statement, click to place a C in the **C** column.

8 When the Balance Difference at the left reaches 0, click **Next**. Click **Finish** at the dialog box that informs you you've balanced your account.

Task 13: Creating a Recurring Transaction

Entering a Transaction that Repeats

Creating *recurring transactions* helps you anticipate and remember when payments are due so you don't mistakenly forget to make one of those payments. A recurring transaction repeats at specified intervals. You use the Bill Calendar to enter and view recurring transactions. After you enter a recurring transaction, the Money 98 Bill Reminder tells you when the next instance of the transaction is coming due. You can then use the Bill Calendar to enter the transaction in the account register, from which you can edit or print the check.

Click

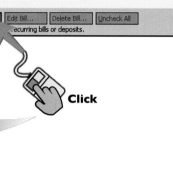

Click

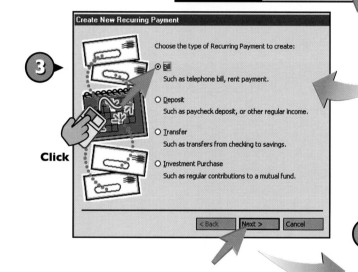

Click

Click

Click **Bills** in the navigation bar.

Click the **New Bill** button in the Bill Calendar screen.

Click the option button for the transaction type you want (**Bill** in this case), then click **Next**.

Review the information in the next dialog box, then click **Next**.

Next Step

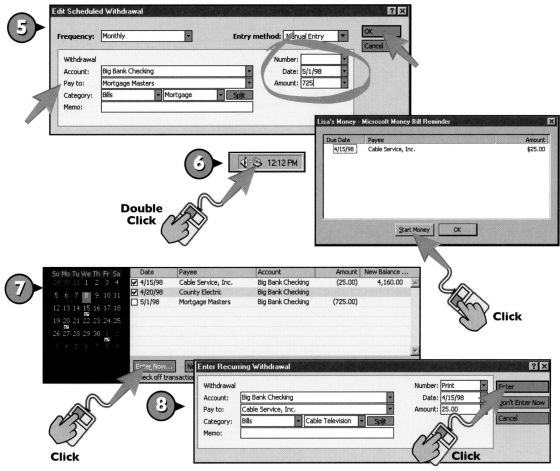

> **WARNING**
> Always make sure you carefully check the amounts for recurring transactions when you reconcile your account. Some transactions, such as pay deposits, can vary by a penny or two at times.

> **Getting Help in Money Dialogs**
> For help on any option in a Money 98 dialog box, click the question mark button in the upper-left corner of the dialog box, then click the option about which you want information.

> **Understanding Other Settings**
> In the Edit Scheduled Withdrawal dialog box, you don't have to enter an amount for recurring transactions. So when such a transaction comes due, you can just plug in the actual amount for the bill you receive. The **Date** entry specifies the date of the first instance of the recurring transaction.

5 ▸ Choose the **Account** for the recurring transaction, fill in the other information about the transaction, and then click **OK**.

6 ▸ If a recurring transaction is due in 10 days or less, the Bill Reminder icon appears when you start your computer. Double-click the **Bill Reminder** icon. Click **Start Money**.

7 ▸ Click to check each recurring transaction that you want to enter in the checking account register, then click **Enter Now**.

8 ▸ Edit the transaction information, such as choosing Print This Transaction from the Number drop-down list or entering an actual bill **Amount**, then click **Enter**.

Task 14: Figuring Your Budget

Budgeting Your Money

Entering payments and other transactions means looking back or dealing with the present. To look ahead, you can use Money to calculate a budget, so you'll know how your income stacks up against your expenses.

✓ **Getting a Head Start**
If you've already entered recurring transactions, that information will be reflected in the initial budget values that appear in the Budget & Savings Plan screen.

ⓘ **WARNING**
If you assign the Net Pay subcategory to your income (paycheck) recurring transactions, they won't show up in your budget. By default, the budget shows only gross pay (before tax and other charges) amounts.

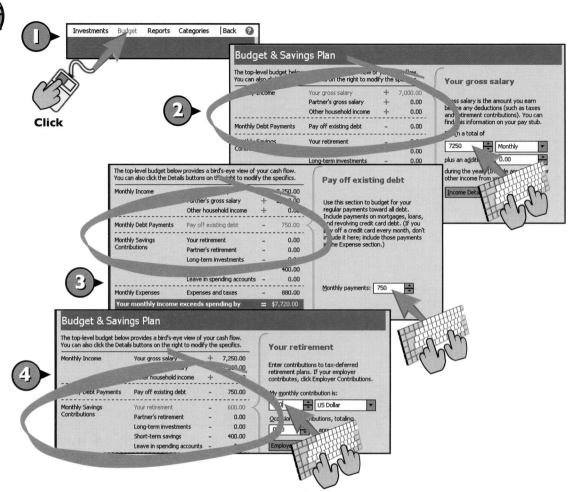

Start Here

Click

Investments Budget Reports Categories │ Back

Budget & Savings Plan

Your gross salary

Pay off existing debt

Your retirement

▶ **1** Click **Budget** in the navigation bar.

▶ **2** For each line in the **Monthly Income** section of the top-level (summary) budget, click the line, then enter the earnings amount and frequency to the right.

▶ **3** Click the **Pay Off Existing Debt** line, then enter the Monthly Payments amount for loans such as mortgages and car payments.

▶ **4** Click each line under Monthly Savings Contribution, then enter the contribution amount(s) to the right.

Next Step

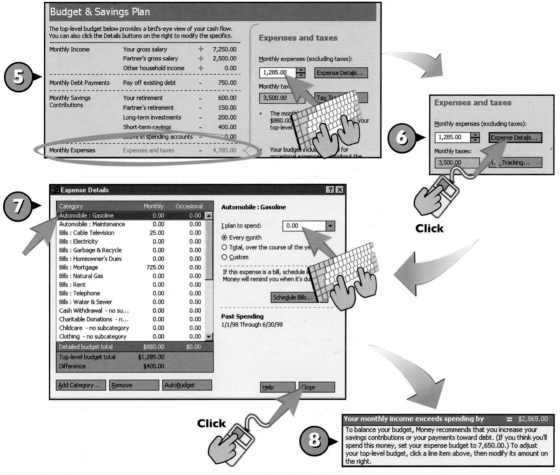

Budget & Savings Plan

The top-level budget below provides a bird's-eye view of your cash flow. You can also click the Details buttons on the right to modify the specifics.

Monthly Income	Your gross salary	+	7,250.00
	Partner's gross salary	+	2,500.00
	Other household income	+	0.00
Monthly Debt Payments	Pay off existing debt	–	750.00
Monthly Savings Contributions	Your retirement	–	600.00
	Partner's retirement	–	150.00
	Long-term investments	–	200.00
	Short-term savings	–	400.00
	Leave in spending accounts	–	0.00
Monthly Expenses	Expenses and taxes	–	4,785.00

Expenses and taxes

Monthly expenses (excluding taxes):

1,285.00   Expense Details...

Monthly taxes:

3,500.00   Tax Tr...

Expenses and taxes

Monthly expenses (excluding taxes):

1,285.00   Expense Details...

Monthly taxes:

3,500.00   ...Tracking...

5

6   Click

Expense Details

Category	Monthly	Occasional
Automobile : Gasoline	0.00	0.00
Automobile : Maintenance	0.00	0.00
Bills : Cable Television	25.00	0.00
Bills : Electricity	0.00	0.00
Bills : Garbage & Recycle	0.00	0.00
Bills : Homeowner's Dues	0.00	0.00
Bills : Mortgage	725.00	0.00
Bills : Natural Gas	0.00	0.00
Bills : Rent	0.00	0.00
Bills : Telephone	0.00	0.00
Bills : Water & Sewer	0.00	0.00
Cash Withdrawal - no su...	0.00	0.00
Charitable Donations - n...	0.00	0.00
Childcare - no subcategory	0.00	0.00
Clothing - no subcategory	0.00	0.00

Detailed budget total	$880.00	$0.00
Top-level budget total	$1,285.00	
Difference	$405.00	

Add Category...   Remove   AutoBudget

Automobile : Gasoline

I plan to spend: 0.00

◉ Every month
○ Total, over the course of the ye
○ Custom

If this expense is a bill, schedule i
Money will remind you when it's du

Schedule Bills...

Past Spending
1/1/98 Through 6/30/98

Help   Close

7

Click

8

Your monthly income exceeds spending by   = $2,865.00

To balance your budget, Money recommends that you increase your savings contributions or your payments toward debt. (If you think you'll spend this money, set your expense budget to 7,650.00.) To adjust your top-level budget, click a line item above, then modify its amount on the right.

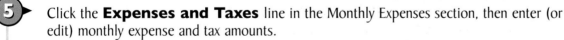

5 Click the **Expenses and Taxes** line in the Monthly Expenses section, then enter (or edit) monthly expense and tax amounts.

6 If you need to provide more detail for a particular line's entry, click the button such as **Income Details**, **Employer Contributions**, or **Expense Details**.

7 Make the needed changes in the resulting dialog box, such as clicking a category and entering an amount for that category, then click **Close**.

8 Review your budget shortfall or surplus and Money's suggestions about it.

✓ **AutoBudgeting**
If you've entered your income and expenses in the account register for some time and have been diligent about categorizing them, you can use the AutoBudget feature to generate a budget for you. To do so, click the **Expenses and Taxes line** in the **Monthly Expenses section of the Budget & Savings Plan screen. Click the Expense Details button, then click the AutoBudget** button in the Expense Details dialog box.

✓ **Redisplaying Your Budget**
The information you enter in the Budget & Savings Plan screen stays there until you delete it or change it. To redisplay that budget information at any time, click **Budget** in the navigation bar.

Creating an Account to Track Investments

Just as you create a separate Money 98 account for each checking or savings account you have, you need to create a separate Money 98 account for each mutual fund or stock investment account you have. Because you have to track some different information when you track investments, such as tracking share prices and dividends, the process for setting up an investment account differs a bit from the process described in Task 3.

✓ Setting Up Numerous Accounts

The best rule of thumb is to create one investment account for each paper investment account statement you receive each month. That way, you can more clearly track your gains and losses in each account, providing helpful information at tax time.

Task 15: Setting Up an Investment Account

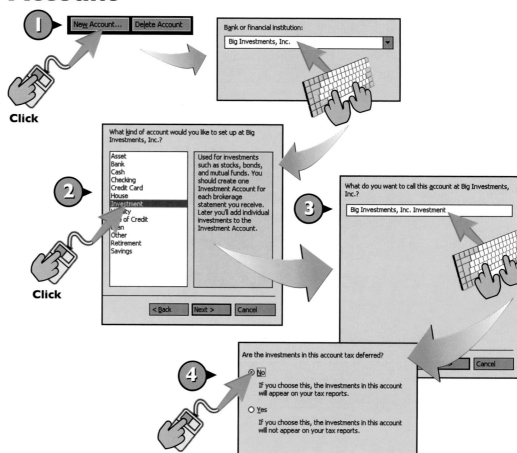

Click

Click

Click

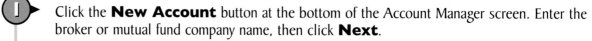

1 Click the **New Account** button at the bottom of the Account Manager screen. Enter the broker or mutual fund company name, then click **Next**.

2 Click **Investment** in the next dialog box, then click **Next**.

3 Edit the suggested account name, if needed, then click **Next**.

4 Click the desired option button to specify whether the investment is tax deferred, then click **Next**.

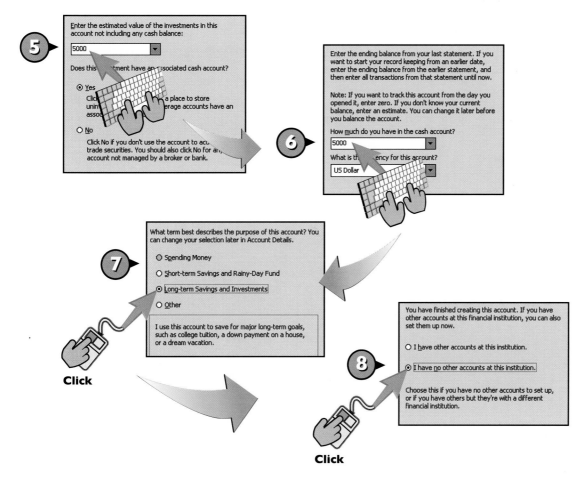

Clarifying Your Initial Entries

If you're starting an investment account from scratch (that is, you've deposited cash in it, but haven't placed any securities trades), enter zero as the estimated investment value and the amount of deposited cash as the current cash value.

Adding Your Account Number

Money doesn't prompt you to enter an account number when you create the investment account, but you can add it later. Right-click the account icon in the Account Manager, then click **Go To Details**. Enter the number in the **Account Number** text box, as well as entering any other details you'd like, then click the **Register** choice at the left to work with the account register.

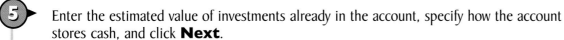

5 ▶ Enter the estimated value of investments already in the account, specify how the account stores cash, and click **Next**.

6 ▶ If the account does hold cash, enter the amount (from the last statement) and click **Next**.

7 ▶ Click the option button that best describes the account's purpose, then click **Next**. Review the information in the next dialog box, then click **Next**.

8 ▶ At the next dialog box, leave **I Have No Other Accounts at this Institution** selected and click **Next**, then click **Finish**.

Entering an Investment Purchase

Each time you buy or sell stock, mutual fund shares, or other investments, or receive a dividend or other distribution that's deposited into your investment account, it's a transaction. You need to enter each transaction into the register for the investment account in Money 98. Entering an investment account transaction resembles doing so in a checking account.

✓ **Entering Other Types of Investments**
This task shows a stock purchase. Obviously, you'll want to choose the right Investment type (stock, mutual fund, and so on) and Activity (Buy, Sell, Dividend deposit, and so on) for each of your transactions, and then enter any additional information that's not specifically covered here.

Task 16: Adding a Stock or Mutual Fund Buy to the Account

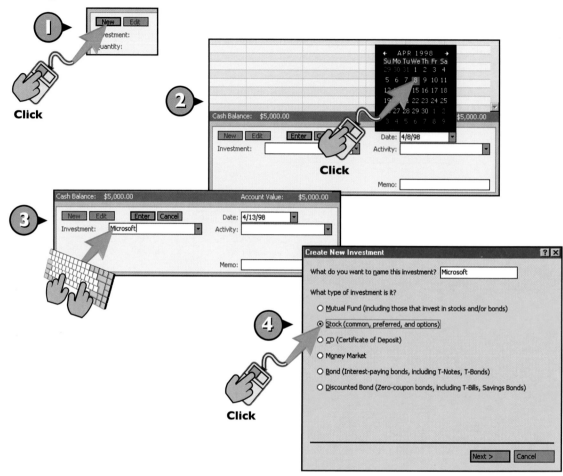

Start Here

Click

Click

Click

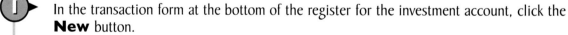

① In the transaction form at the bottom of the register for the investment account, click the **New** button.

② Click the drop-down list arrow beside the **Date** text box, click the date for the check in the calendar that appears, then press **Tab**.

③ Enter the name of the stock or mutual fund in the **Investment** text box, then click the drop-down list arrow beside the **Activity** text box.

④ Verify the investment name, click the option button for the investment type for the transaction, then click **Next**.

Next Step

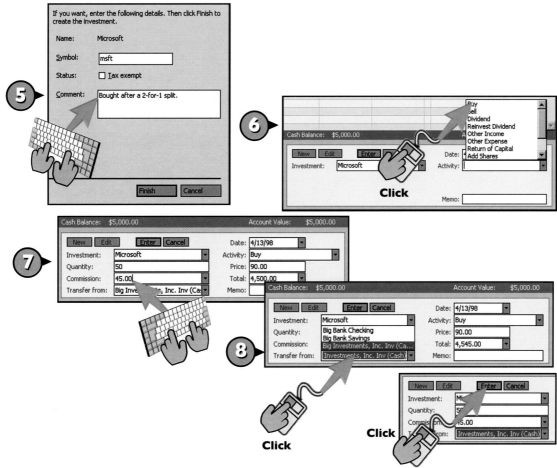

Page
143

Opening the Investment Account Register

To open the register for your investment account, double-click the **Accounts** button on the navigation bar to redisplay the Account Manager. Then, double-click the icon for the investment account.

Already-Identified Investments

Steps 4 and 5 apply only if you haven't previously entered a transaction for a particular investment (a particular stock or mutual fund, for example).

Moving between Cash and Investments

When your brokerage account stores both investments and cash, Money tracks the cash portion of the account in a separate register linked to the main investment account. To move to the register tracking cash, click **Cash Account** in the lower-left corner of the main investment account register.

5 ▶ Specify the stock ticker **Symbol**, **Status**, and **Comment**. Click **Finish**.

6 ▶ In the open Activity list, click the correct transaction activity.

7 ▶ Enter the Quantity (number of shares), Price (per share or unit), and Commission (broker's fee amount) in the appropriate text boxes.

8 ▶ Change the **Transfer From** (or Transfer To) account, if needed. Click the **Enter** button on the transaction form to enter the transaction in the register.

Task 17: Backing Up Your Money File

Creating a Backup Money File

Money 98 automatically asks you whether you want to back up the open file when you exit Money. However, that doesn't prevent you from losing information if there's a power fluctuation that reboots your computer without warning, or if some other catastrophe occurs. So make a habit of backing up your Money file every 10 minutes or so.

✓ **Using the Backup File**
Backing up saves a copy of the Money file with exactly the information it held when you completed the backup process. If your current file won't open and you need to use that backup data, choose **File, Restore Backup**. If the file to restore doesn't appear in the **Restore File From** text box of the Restore Backup dialog box, click the **Browse** button, select the file in the Restore dialog box, then click **OK**.

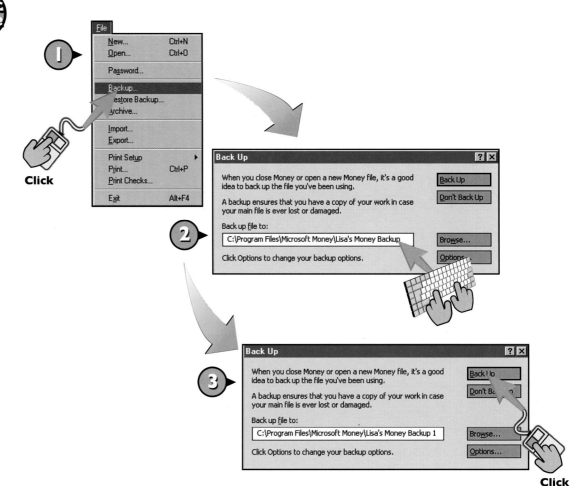

Start Here

Click

Click

1. Choose **File**, **Backup**.

2. If you want to specify an alternate name or location for the backup file, edit the **Back Up File To** text box entry.

3. Click the **Back Up** button.

End Task

Task 18: Opening Another Money File

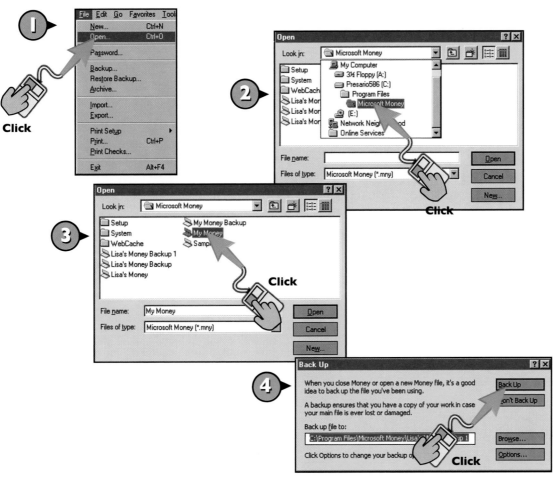

Start Here

Click

1

2

3

Click

4

Click

Choosing the Money File to Use

Task 2 explained how to create a new Money file to separate the financial data for each Money user. Since then, the tasks have assumed you were working in the correct Money file. When the time comes to switch users, you can open the needed Money file, as described in this task.

✓ **New Year, New File**
If your finances are simple and you don't use the budgeting or reports features in Money, you also can create a new Money file each year. When you need to refer to the prior year's file, you can open it.

✓ **Adding Password Protection**
You can add a password for any Money file to control which household members may open the file. Choose the **File, Password** command, enter the password in the **New Password** text box, then click **OK**.

1 ▶ Choose **File**, **Open**.

2 ▶ If needed, use the Look In drop-down list to select the disk and folder that holds the file.

3 ▶ Click the file to open in the list of files in the Open dialog box. Click the **Open** button.

4 ▶ Click **Back Up** to back up the previously opened Money file before it closes.

End Task

Browsing the Web with Internet Explorer

Web browser software enables you to look at information posted in special locations on the Internet. Web browsers display information that has attractive formatting and includes sounds, animated pictures, and more. The information you view via your Web browser can excite and entertain you, as well as inform you. This part shows you how to use Internet Explorer 3.02, the browser that comes with Home Essentials, to view and find information online.

Tasks

Task 1: Launching and Exiting Internet Explorer

Launching and Exiting Internet Explorer

The *World Wide Web* (the *Web*), a collection of computers on the Internet, stores and presents information graphically. To view Web information, you use *Web browser* software. Microsoft Home Essentials 98 includes the Internet Explorer 3.02 Web browser. When you launch Internet Explorer, it prompts you to use your computer modem to dial your Internet connection with an *Internet service provider* (ISP).

WARNING

Windows 98 includes Internet Explorer 4.0. The steps for using Explorer 4.0 are essentially the same as those for using Explorer 3.02, described in this part. Your Explorer 4.0 screen may look slightly different than those pictured here, however.

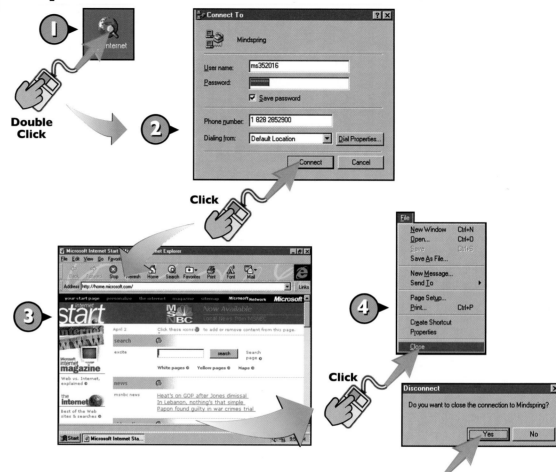

Start Here

Double Click

Click

Click

1 Double-click the **Internet** icon on the desktop.

2 Click **Connect** in the Connect To dialog box to dial your Internet connection.

3 When Internet Explorer appears, you can read the initial page and display other information (see Tasks 2–8).

4 Choose **File**, **Close** when you're finished viewing Web information. Click **Yes** to disconnect from the Internet.

End Task

Task 2: Using a URL to Jump to a Web Page

Start Here

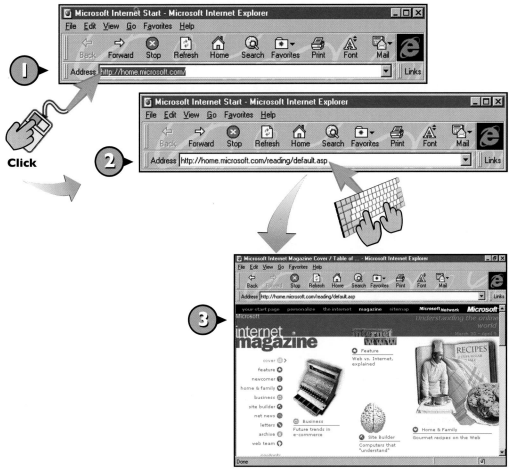

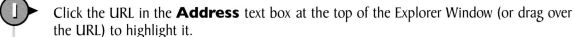

① Click the URL in the **Address** text box at the top of the Explorer Window (or drag over the URL) to highlight it.

② Type the URL of the page to view and press **Enter**.

③ When the Web page appears, you can read it or browse to other pages.

Using a URL

The Web stores information in Web pages. The Web identifies each Web page with a *Web address* called the *Uniform Resource Locator (URL)*. Each Web URL consists of the *content identifier*, `http://`, which identifies the address as a Web address. The rest of the address, its location, identifies the Web site (`www.microsoft.com`), directory (`/games/`), and a page name (`default.htm`), which is optional. So, a full Web address may look like `http://www.microsoft.com/games/default.htm`. To display a particular Web page (called *browsing*), you can enter its address in Internet Explorer.

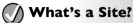 **What's a Site?**
A Web site is a particular computer (or designated storage area on such a computer) that holds Web pages and is connected to the Internet.

Using a Link

In addition to interesting text and graphics, Web pages offer *links* (or *hyperlinks*) to other Web pages. Click the link to jump to the page it represents instead of remembering and typing a URL. A link can be text, highlighted with a special color or underlining, or a button or graphic on the page. After you use a link to display a particular page and then return to the page that holds that link, Explorer changes the link text's color or perhaps adds a border around a link button so that you can tell which links you've already followed.

✓ Finding Links

If you're not sure whether highlighted text or a graphic represents a link, point to it with the mouse. If it's a link, the pointer changes to a hand. The status bar displays the Web address (or a shortcut for that address).

Task 3: Clicking a Link to Display Another Page

Start Here

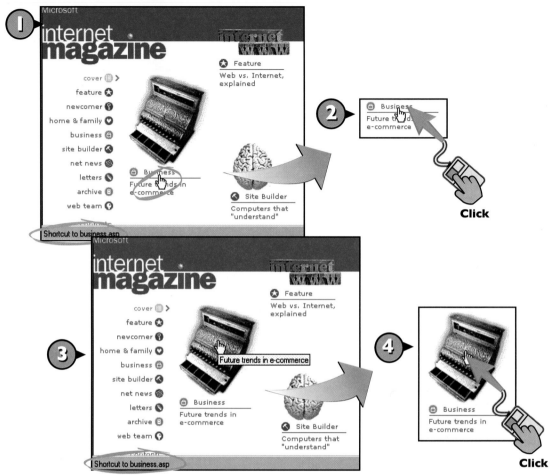

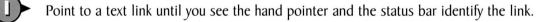

1 ▶ Point to a text link until you see the hand pointer and the status bar identify the link.

2 ▶ Click the text link to display the linked page.

3 ▶ Point to a linked graphic until you see the hand pointer, and the status bar and a description identify the link.

4 ▶ Click the linked graphic to display the linked page.

End Task

Task 4: Backing Up or Going Forward

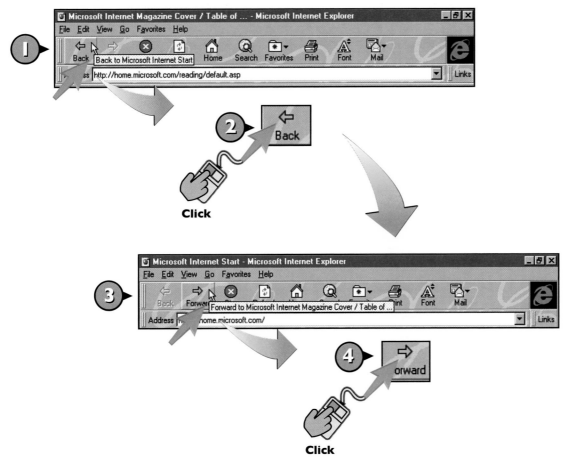

The Back and Forward buttons in Internet Explorer work somewhat like the Rewind and Fast Forward on a VCR. Click the **Back** button to return to a page you've previously viewed. Click **Back** multiple times to move back through several successive pages. Click the **Forward** button to redisplay successive pages in the order in which you originally displayed them. Using Back and Forward is easier than remembering which links you used or typing various URLs.

✓ **Skipping to Another Page**
If you want to jump directly to a page rather than backing up or moving forward through multiple pages, click the drop-down list arrow beside the Address drop-down list and click the URL for the page you want.

① To move back, point to the **Back** button to see a pop-up description of the previous page.

② Click the **Back** button to redisplay the previous page.

③ To move forward, point to the **Forward** button to see a pop-up description of the next page.

④ Click the **Forward** button to redisplay the next page.

Adding a Favorite Page

You can mark a Web page you use often so that you can quickly display it at any time. You create a shortcut, called a favorite, that you can select to jump to the page rather than entering the URL. The favorite represents the Web page's URL. Explorer stores the favorites on the Favorites menu or in the Favorites list that appears when you click the Favorites toolbar button.

ⓘ WARNING

Don't bother adding a page with a short lifespan to your list of Favorites, such as an article from an online magazine. Instead, choose **File, Save As File** and use the Save In list to specify a disk and folder to save the file to, enter a name for the file in the **File Name** text box, then click **Save**. This saves the article as an HTML file (a Web page file) on your hard disk.

Task 5: Adding a Page to Your List of Favorites

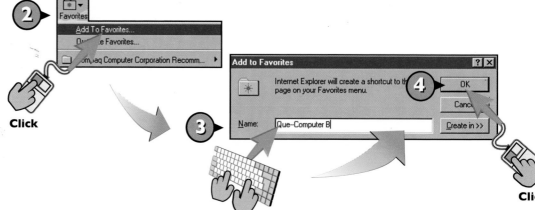

Click

Click

① ▶ Display the Web page that you want to mark as a favorite page.

② ▶ Click the **Favorites** button and then **Add to Favorites**. (In Explorer 4.0, choose **Favorites**, **Add to Favorites**.)

③ ▶ If needed, type a name for the favorite in the **Name** text box. This name appears on the Favorites menu or list.

④ ▶ Click **OK** to finish adding the favorite to your list.

Task 6: Displaying a Favorite Page

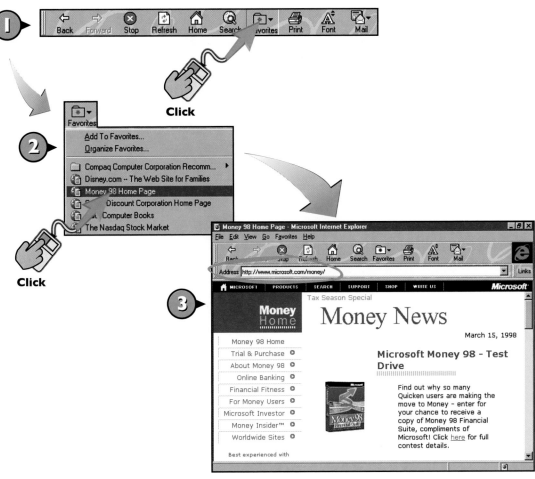

Click

Click

Displaying a Favorite Page

After you've marked a favorite page as described in Task 5, the name you specified for the favorite appears on the Favorites menu and the list that appears when you click the Favorites button.

✓ **Handling an Obsolete Favorite**
If a favorite no longer works because the Web page has been deleted or its address has changed, you can delete the favorite. See Task 7, "Organizing Your Favorites," to see how to delete a favorite.

✓ **Grouping Your Favorites**
You can store your favorites in specific folders to organize favorites by topic, such as Health, Finances, or Games. See Task 7 to learn how to create folders and move favorites into them.

1 Click the **Favorites** button or **Favorites** menu.

2 Click the name of the favorite page you want to display in the list or menu. (In Explorer 4.0, the Favorites list appears at the left.)

3 When the favorite page appears, you can review it, click links, or display another page.

End Task

Task 7: Organizing Your Favorites

Organizing Your Favorites

If you add numerous favorites to your list, the list can become quite lengthy. Scanning through a list of 40 favorites could take as much time as entering a URL. To ensure that your favorites continue to save you time, you can create folders to group the favorites by topic, such as Health, Finances, Cars, Crafts, and so on. Placing your favorites into folders gives you more control over how Explorer lists the favorites. The Favorites list displays each folder name; select the folder to display the favorites you've placed in that folder.

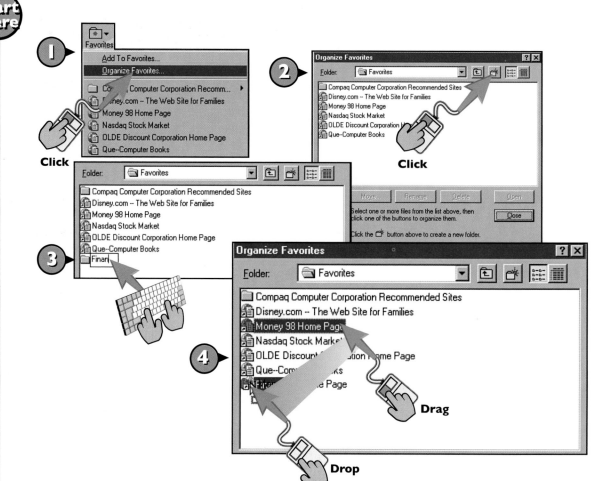

✓ Tweaking Your Favorites List

By default, Explorer lists your favorites in alphabetical order. You can edit the name of a favorite to ensure it's listed as you prefer.

1 Click the **Favorites** button and then click **Organize Favorites**. (Choose **Favorites**, **Organize Favorites** in Explorer 4.0.)

2 Click the **Create New Folder** button.

3 Type a new folder name, which appears beside the folder icon, then press **Enter**.

4 Drag a favorite and drop it on the folder icon to move the favorite into that folder.

Next Step

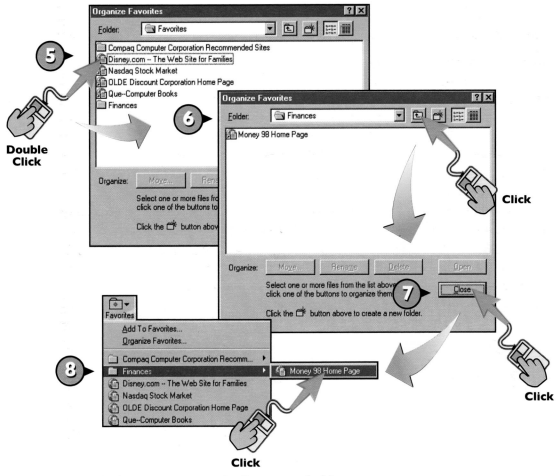

Double Click

Click

Click

Click

Click

✓ **Deleting a Favorite**
You can delete an old favorite by using the **Organize Favorites** dialog box. Click the name of the Favorite to delete, and then click the **Delete** button.

✓ **Selecting Multiple Favorites**
To select multiple folders or favorites in the **Organize Favorites** dialog box, press and hold the **Ctrl** key and click the icon for each folder or favorite to select.

5 ▸ Double-click a folder's icon to view the favorites it holds.

6 ▸ Click the **Up One Level** button to move up one level in the folder list (back to the main Favorites list, in most cases).

7 ▸ Click the **Close** button to finish organizing favorites.

8 ▸ Click the **Favorites** button, point to a folder name to display its favorites, then click the favorite to display. (Click a folder in Explorer 4.0 to list its favorites.)

End Task

Task 8: Searching for Information

Using a Search

There are millions of Web pages, so Internet Explorer offers a built-in way to use your choice of several search tools offered on the Web. Independent companies operate these search tools, such as Yahoo!, Excite, Lycos, AOL NetFind, and InfoSeek. Enter the *search words* (topic) you want to find, and the search tool searches its catalog of registered pages and lists the matching pages. Click a listed page to display it in Explorer.

✓ Fine-Tuning Your Search

If you enter more than one search word, as in "organic gardening," most search tools list Web pages that contain any of the search words. To display only pages that contain all the search words you enter, type quotation marks around the search words or use a plus sign or AND between them.

Start Here

Click

Click

① Click the **Search** button. (It doesn't matter what Web page is currently displayed.)

② Type your search word(s) in the search text box of the search tool that appears.

③ Click the **Search** button. (This button may be named Seek for some search tools.)

Next Step

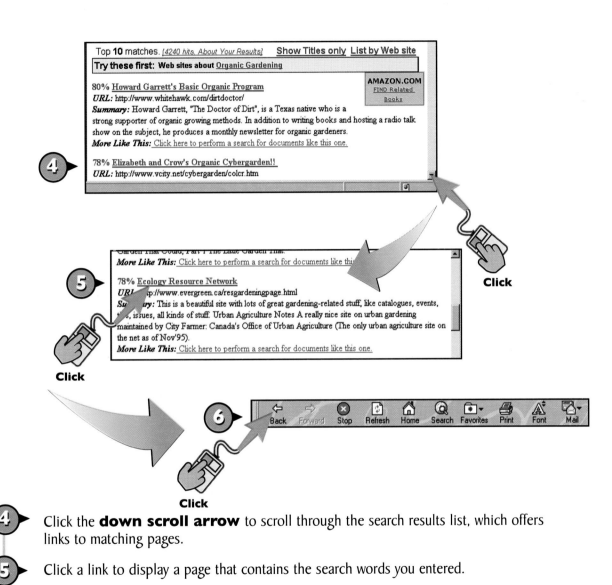

Top **10** matches. *[4240 hits, About Your Results]*   Show Titles only List by Web site

Try these first: Web sites about <u>Organic Gardening</u>

80% <u>Howard Garrett's Basic Organic Program</u>
URL: http://www.whitehawk.com/dirtdoctor/
Summary: Howard Garrett, "The Doctor of Dirt", is a Texas native who is a strong supporter of organic growing methods. In addition to writing books and hosting a radio talk show on the subject, he produces a monthly newsletter for organic gardeners.
More Like This: <u>Click here to perform a search for documents like this one.</u>

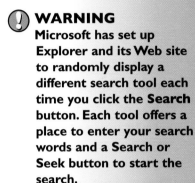
AMAZON.COM
FIND Related
Books

78% <u>Elizabeth and Crow's Organic Cybergarden!!</u>
URL: http://www.vcity.net/cybergarden/colcr.htm

Garden That Could, Part 1 The Little Garden That.
More Like This: <u>Click here to perform a search for documents like this</u>

78% <u>Ecology Resource Network</u>
URL: http://www.evergreen.ca/resgardeningpage.html
Summary: This is a beautiful site with lots of great gardening-related stuff, like catalogues, events, t's, issues, all kinds of stuff. Urban Agriculture Notes A really nice site on urban gardening maintained by City Farmer: Canada's Office of Urban Agriculture (The only urban agriculture site on the net as of Nov'95).
More Like This: <u>Click here to perform a search for documents like this one.</u>

Click

Click

← → ✕ 🗘 🏠 🔍 📷▾ 🖨 🗛 📧▾
Back Forward Stop Refresh Home Search Favorites Print Font Mail

Click

Click

④ ▸ Click the **down scroll arrow** to scroll through the search results list, which offers links to matching pages.

⑤ ▸ Click a link to display a page that contains the search words you entered.

⑥ ▸ Click the **Back** button to return to the search results list.

ⓘ **WARNING**
Microsoft has set up Explorer and its Web site to randomly display a different search tool each time you click the **Search** button. Each tool offers a place to enter your search words and a Search or Seek button to start the search.

✓ **Using Your Favorite Search Tool**
To display your favorite search tool, type its URL in the Address text box and press Enter. (You may also add it to your list of Favorites.) Search tools offer a variety of different features and types of information, such as classified ads; entertainment news; address, phone number, and email listings; and more.

End Task

Task 9: Downloading a File

Downloading a File

The free stuff available on the Internet has contributed to the explosion of folks signing online. To attract you to a Web site, its publisher may offer files you can download, such as research documents, software, sound files, or graphics. Software publishers such as Microsoft often use a Web site as a place to post downloadable patches that fix glitches in a particular software version. It's easy to use a link to download the file and save it to your hard disk.

✓ How Explorer Transfers Files

The Internet uses a communication method called *FTP (file transfer protocol)* to transfer files to your system from a Web site. Until a year or two ago, you had to use separate FTP software to retrieve files. Now, Internet Explorer handles that job.

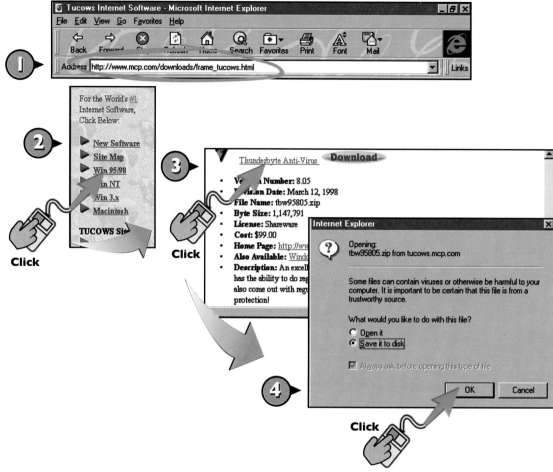

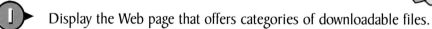

Display the Web page that offers categories of downloadable files.

Click links, if needed, to navigate to the category that holds the file to download.

Click the link or button for the file to download.

Leave **Save It to Disk** selected in the dialog box that appears and click **OK**.

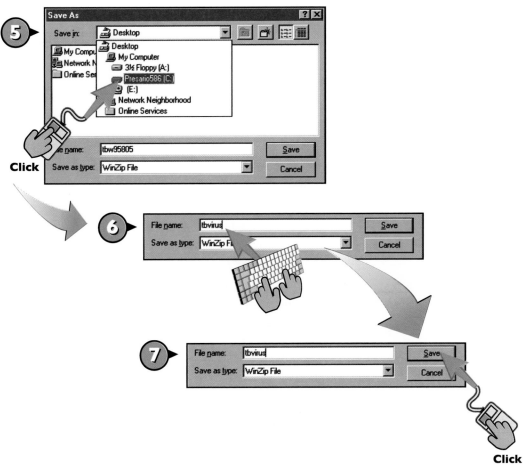

Click

Click

WARNING
Any file you download from the Web (Internet) could be infected with a computer *virus*, a program designed to alter how your computer works or even damage information on your system. If you plan to download files often, you should purchase and install an anti-virus program such as **McAfee VirusScan, Thunderbyte Antivirus**, or **Norton Antivirus**.

Sharing the Software Load
If you download software from the Web, it's generally not free. Most software on the Web is *shareware.* You can download the shareware to test it out, but you need to send a modest payment to the shareware author. Shareware works on the honor system, so please do your part and pay your shareware fees.

5 ▶ Choose a disk (and folder) to save the file to from the **Save In** list.

6 ▶ Edit the filename, if needed.

7 ▶ Click **Save**. After the file downloads, the File Download dialog box closes on its own.

End Task

Displaying the Home Essentials Site

The **Microsoft Home Essentials Site** doesn't reside on the **Web**. Instead, it's a file stored in the **Web** file format (.htm) on the first **CD-ROM** (Disc 1) in the Home Essentials 98 set of **CD-ROM**s. Because the file is in the **Web** file format, you can display the file in Explorer. The Home Essentials Site (file) offers links just like regular **Web** pages. You can click a link to go to other pages stored on the **CD-ROM** or pages stored on the **Web**.

Task 10: Displaying the Home Essentials Site

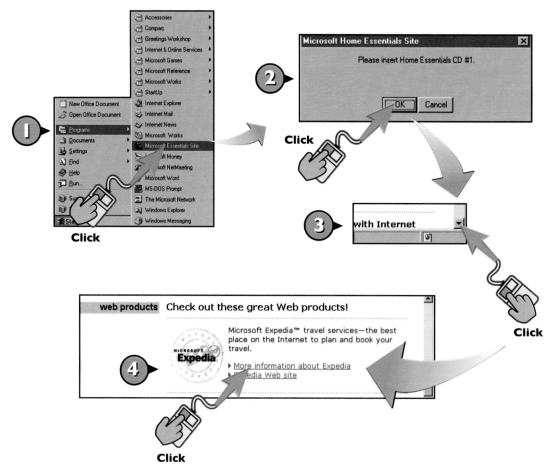

> ⓘ **WARNING**
> If the Home Essentials Setup program runs automatically when you insert the **CD-ROM**, click the **Exit Setup** button to close it.

1 Click **Start**, point to **Programs**, then click **Microsoft Essentials Site**.

2 When prompted, insert the Home Essentials CD #1 in your CD-ROM drive and click **OK** if the dialog box doesn't close.

3 Click the **down scroll arrow** to scroll through the site information.

4 Click a link to display a page with more information about the link topic.

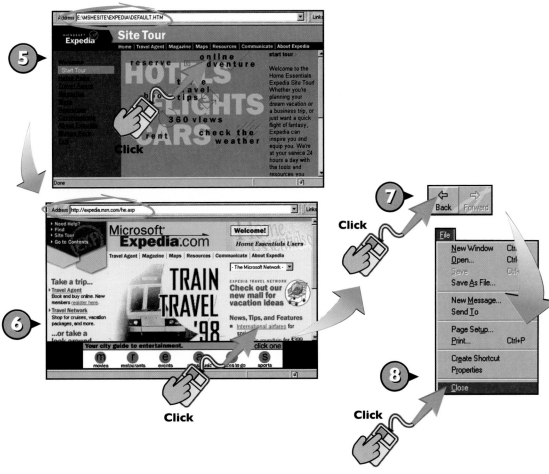

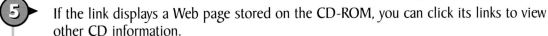

Click

Click

Click

7

8

5

6

5 ▶ If the link displays a Web page stored on the CD-ROM, you can click its links to view other CD information.

6 ▶ If the link displays a page on Microsoft's Web site, you can click its links to view other online information.

7 ▶ Click the **Back** button to back up to other pages as needed.

8 ▶ Choose **File, Close** to finish, then remove the CD-ROM from your drive.

WARNING
If you're not presently connected to the Internet and click a link on the Home Essentials site that leads to a page on Microsoft's Web site, the Connect To dialog box appears. Click the Connect button in that dialog box to dial your Internet connection so the linked Web page can display.

WARNING
If you're connected to the Internet when you choose File, Close, a dialog box asks if you want to disconnect. Click Yes to do so.

End Task

PART 5

Exploring Education and Entertainment Features

Part of the beauty of having a computer at home is that you can use it for any purpose that your time and software allow. Home Essentials offers two applications that enable you to explore how to use your computer for fun and education. This part shows you how to use Greetings Workshop to create cards, party decorations, and more. The part also demonstrates how you and your children can use the Encarta 98 Encyclopedia to explore history.

Tasks

Launching Greetings Workshop

How many times have you or your children spent hours with paper and markers to make cards, posters, or party banners? In many cases, such projects provide a great family activity. In other cases, you may want a faster method or more polished results. You can create a number of colorful projects in Greetings Workshop. This task explains how to start the program and begin working.

Task 1: Starting and Logging On to Greetings Workshop

Start Here

Double Click

Click

✓ **Logging On Again**
If you've previously logged on and entered your user name, click your name in the list that appears to log on and finish starting Greetings Workshop.

① ▶ Double-click the **Greetings Workshop** shortcut on the Windows Desktop.

② ▶ Click the **Add a Name** button.

③ ▶ Enter your first name.

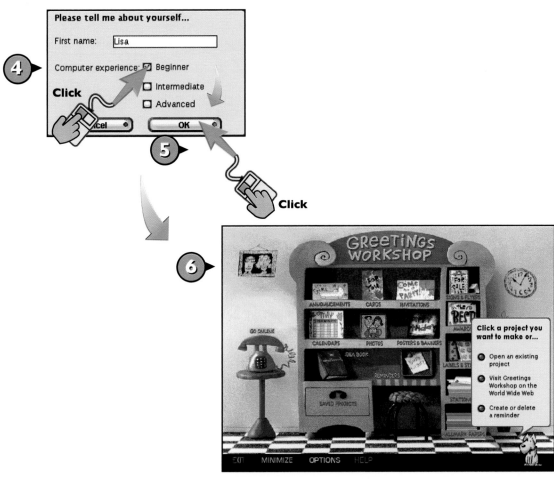

4 Click the button for your **Computer Experience Level**.

5 Click **OK**.

6 Begin your work in Greetings Workshop.

✓ **Using the Start Menu, Instead**
You also can use the Start menu to launch Greetings Workshop. Click **Start**, point to **Programs**, then to **Greetings Workshop**, and then click **Greetings Workshop**.

Designing a New Project

Most applications open a blank file for you. Because the types of projects you can create in Greetings Workshop vary so dramatically, you have to tell the program right off the bat what kind of project (file) you want to create. After you follow the steps described here, you'll need to continue with the next few tasks to specify the project's contents and adjust how it looks.

⚠ WARNING
The tasks in this book depict creating a greeting card. The specific steps for different types of projects vary. However, the techniques you learn for working with text and pictures apply in any project you create.

Task 2: Creating a Project and Choosing a Design

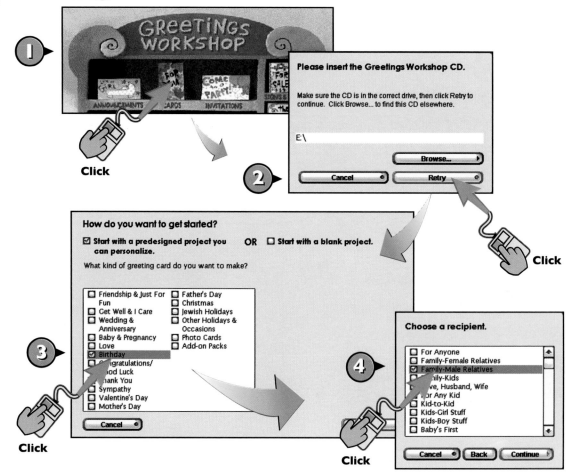

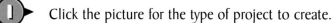

① ▶ Click the picture for the type of project to create.

② ▶ Insert the Greetings Workshop CD-ROM (Disc 2) in your CD-ROM drive and click the **Retry** button.

③ ▶ Click to choose a more specific type of project (card) to create and click **Continue**.

④ ▶ If prompted, click a recipient in the list, and then click **Continue**.

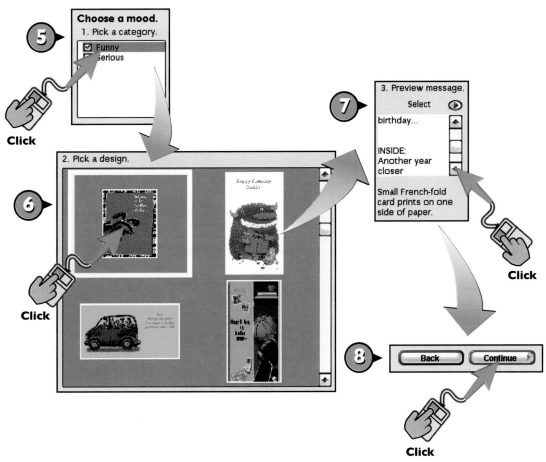

Choose a mood.
1. Pick a category.
- ☑ Funny
- ☐ Serious

Click

2. Pick a design.

Click

Click

3. Preview message.
Select ▶

birthday...

INSIDE:
Another year closer

Small French-fold card prints on one side of paper.

Click

Back Continue ▶

Click

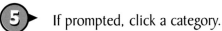

5 If prompted, click a category.

6 Scroll through the design choices and click the design you want.

7 Scroll to review the card message, if you want.

8 Click **Continue**.

✓ **Creating Subsequent Projects**
After you create and save your first project, click the **New Project** button in the upper-left corner of the Greetings Workshop screen to return to the screen that displays the types of new projects you can create.

✓ **Closing Tip Bubbles**
Any time you see a message or tip bubble in Greetings Workshop (other than ones from the helpful dog in the lower-right corner of the screen), you can click anywhere in the bubble to close it.

End Task

Task 3: Personalizing the Message

Entering Project Content

Unless your card recipient and interior message (or the text in another type of project) happens to match the name and text you need, you must edit it. Greetings Workshop presents the opportunity to do so immediately after you create the project and choose its mood and design.

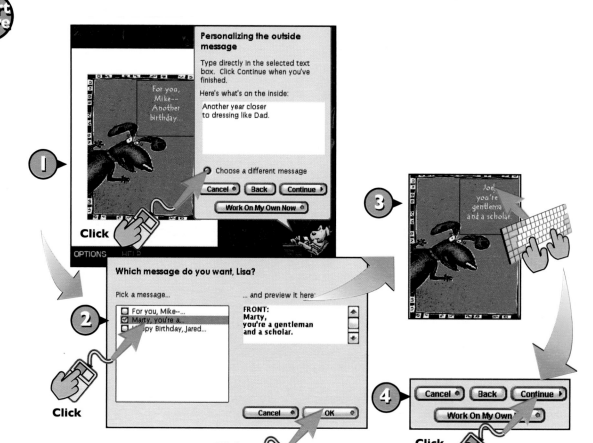

① If you want to use another message entirely for the front of the card, click **Choose a Different Message**.

② Click the message you want, then click **OK**.

③ Click in the text box for the card's front page and edit to enter the new recipient name.

④ Click **Continue**.

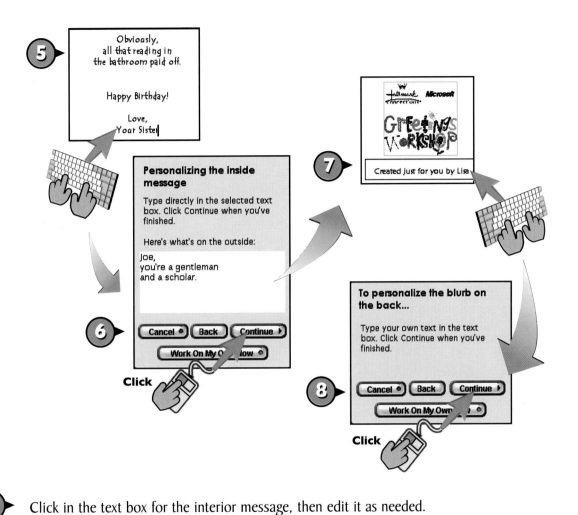

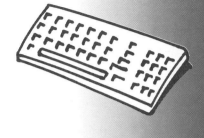

Manually Entering Information
You can click the **Work on My Own Now** button at any time to skip the steps for personalizing the message.

Making Your Changes
Even if you don't nail your text down the first time through, you can edit it later. See Task 5, "Editing Page Text," to learn how.

(5) Click in the text box for the interior message, then edit it as needed.

(6) Click **Continue**.

(7) If needed, click in the blurb text box and edit its contents.

(8) Click **Continue** to finish entering Page text.

Task 4: Selecting a Page or Zoom

Viewing Project Information

After you select the look and text for your card or other project, you can work with particular elements such as blocks of text or graphics. You can zoom in to get a closer look at what you're working with, then zoom back out to see the results. In addition, you can display a particular page. The buttons along the left side of the Greetings Workshop screen enable you to change the view and zoom.

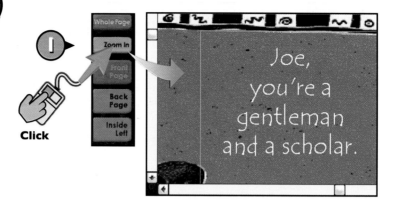

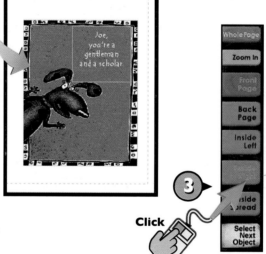

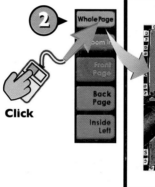

Different Projects, Different Views
The available views depend on the type of project you created. For example, several different projects don't have multiple pages.

1 Click the **Zoom In** button to zoom in on the current page.

2 Click the **Whole Page** button to zoom back out.

3 Click the button for the page (or the view of multiple pages) you want.

Task 5: Editing Page Text

Start Here

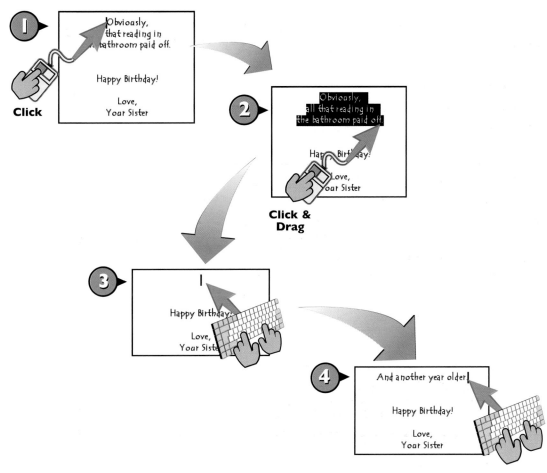

Click

Click & Drag

Changing the Text in a Project

Greetings Workshop places text in predefined text boxes. If you've edited text in a word processor such as Word 97, you can use many of the same techniques in Greetings Workshop. This task covers the most basic editing tasks.

✓ **Cutting and Copying**
The top of the Greetings Workshop screen offers Cut, Copy, and Paste buttons to move or copy text. These buttons work just like those in Word 97. See Tasks 7 and 8 to learn how to move and copy text.

✓ **What Are Those Buttons?**
When you click in a text box, buttons for formatting the text appear. Task 6, "Changing the Look of Page Text," explains how to work with these buttons.

1️⃣ Click in the text box to position the insertion point in it.

2️⃣ Drag over text to select it.

3️⃣ Press **Delete** to delete it.

4️⃣ Type new text to insert it at the insertion point.

Task 6: Changing the Look of Page Text

Formatting Text

Each text box in the project you create uses text formatting meant to complement the design you selected for the project. That doesn't prevent you from doing your own thing, though. For example, if you enter very little text in a text box, you may want to make the text larger. You can apply another font and size to the text: Make it bold, italic, or underlined; change it to outline-style; add a drop-shadow; change the alignment within the box; or change the color.

✓ **Formatting Only Certain Words**
You also can select text within a text box and apply text formatting only to that selection.

✓ **Pressing the Buttons**
When you click a button to apply formatting to text, a blue outline appears around the button. To remove the formatting (and the outline around the button), click the button again.

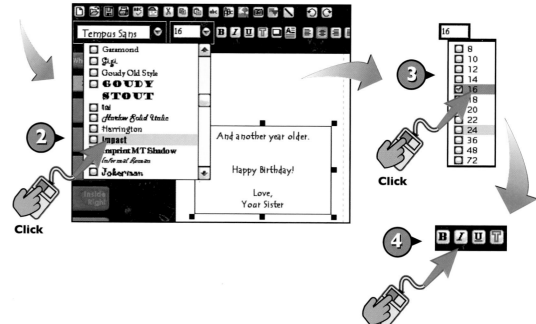

1 ▶ Click the border of the text box to select the whole box and display the buttons for formatting text.

2 ▶ Open the **Change Font Type** drop-down list, scroll it, and click a new font for the text.

3 ▶ Open the **Change Font Size** drop-down list and click the font size to use.

4 ▶ To toggle Bold, Italic, Underline, or Outline on or off, click the button for that effect.

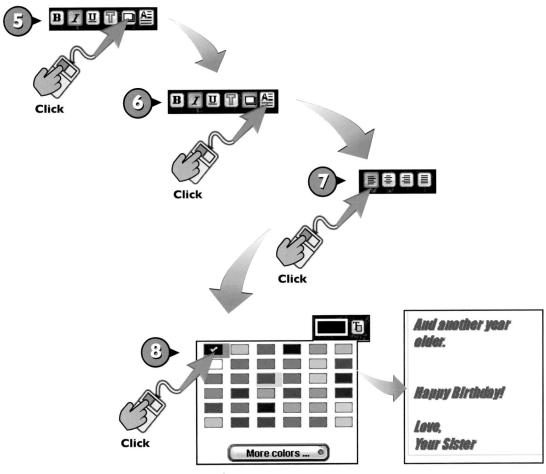

✓ **Expanding Text Boxes**
When you make text larger, the text box holding it automatically expands in size.

✓ **Getting Help from Rocky**
The little dog who gives you help throughout Greetings Workshop is named Rocky. (You can click on him to pet him.) When you click in a text box, Rocky presents buttons for adding a fancy effect to a text box, such as rotating the box.

5 To add a shadow, click the **Shadow** button.

6 To make the first letter a large initial capital, click the **Big First Letter** button.

7 To change the alignment of the text, click an alignment button (Left Align, Center, Right Align, or Justify).

8 To choose another text color, click the **Change Color** button, and then click a new color in the palette that appears. Click outside the text box to finish your changes.

Task 7: Adding a Picture to a Page

Inserting a Greetings Workshop Picture

The Word 97 and Works 4.5 programs call the predrawn pictures you can insert clip art. Greetings Workshop calls its predrawn images pictures. Most project designs include one or two pictures, but not necessarily on each page. For example, a greeting card you're creating typically will include a picture on the front, but may not include a picture on the interior page with your message. You can add a picture to that message page to make it even more colorful and interesting.

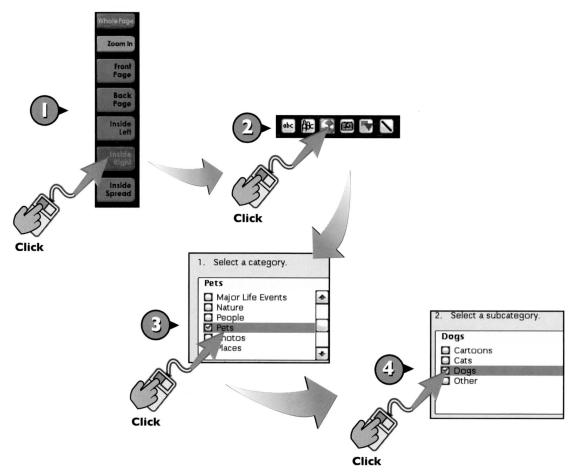

1 Display the page where you want to insert a picture.

2 Click the **Add New Picture** button.

3 Click a picture category.

4 Click a picture subcategory.

Next Step

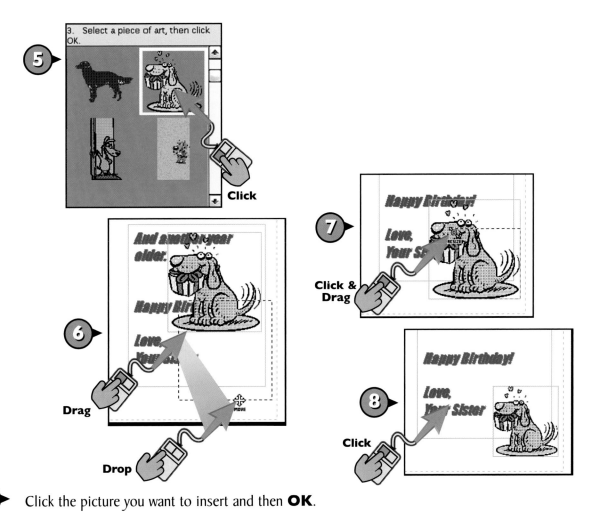

5 Click the picture you want to insert and then **OK**.

6 Point to the picture border until you see the Move pointer, then drag the picture to a new location.

7 Point to a corner handle on the picture border until you see the Resize pointer, then drag the corner to resize the picture.

8 Click outside the picture to deselect it.

✓ **Choosing a Better Picture**
If you plan to print your project on a black and white printer, choose a black and white picture to ensure the best quality. While your black and white printer can print the color pictures, in some cases the pictures may lose detail and clarity when converted from color to black and white.

Inserting Your Own Photos

Digital cameras enable you to store pictures on disk rather than film. You can then print these images with your color printer. To personalize your projects in Greetings Workshop, you can insert a photo of your child or pet that you've snapped with your digital camera. Greetings Workshop also considers graphics you've drawn in a program such as Windows Paint as "photos." In fact, you can insert any "photo" in the .bmp, .pcx, .tif, or a number of other graphics formats into a Greetings Workshop project.

✓ **Deleting Pictures and Photos**

To delete any picture or photo from a page, click it to display a black border with selection handles. Press **Delete**.

Task 8: Adding a Photo to a Page

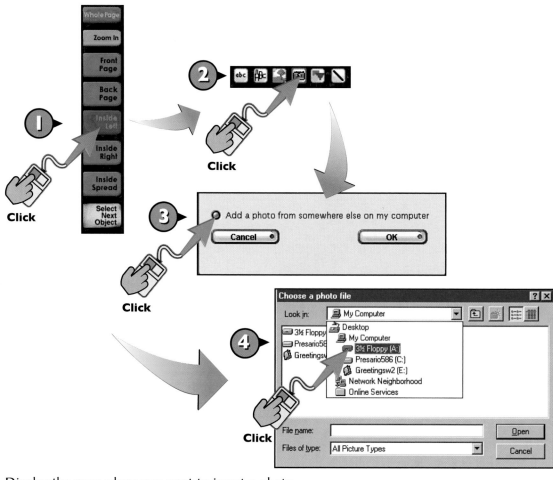

Click

Click

Click

Click

① Display the page where you want to insert a photo.

② Click the **Add New Photo** button.

③ Click **Add a Photo from Somewhere Else on My Computer**.

④ Use the **Look In** drop-down list to navigate to the disk and folder that holds the photo you want to insert.

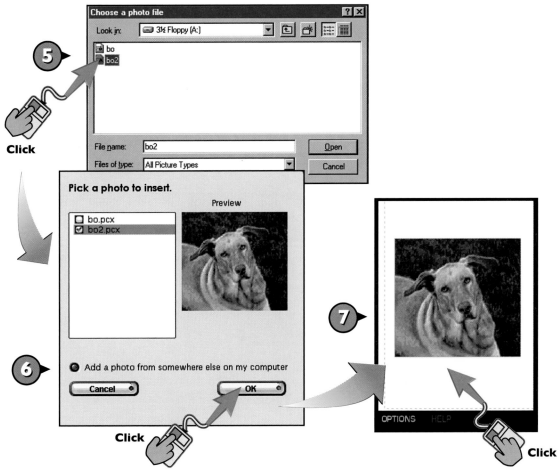

Click

Click

Click

End
Task

WARNING
If the photo you want to insert is on a floppy disk, make sure you insert the disk in the drive or copy the image to your hard disk before starting this process so that Greetings Workshop can find the photo.

Finding Stored Photos
After you insert the first photo, the next time you click the **Add New Photo** button, Greetings Workshop lists the photos in the disk and folder you previously specified. You can click the **Add a Photo from Somewhere Else on My Computer** button to choose another disk and folder.

Making Your Photos Digital
Even if you don't have your own digital camera, many local and national photo development companies will scan your photos and provide them on disk.

5 ▶ Click the photo you want to insert, then click **Open**.

6 ▶ Double-check the preview to verify you've selected the right photo, then click **OK**.

7 ▶ After you drag a corner to resize the picture or a side handle to move it, click outside the picture to finish.

Task 9: Saving a Project

Saving Your Work

Saving a project in Greetings Workshop resembles saving a project in other applications. When you save, you name the project file and specify where to store it on disk so that you can later open, edit, and print it as needed.

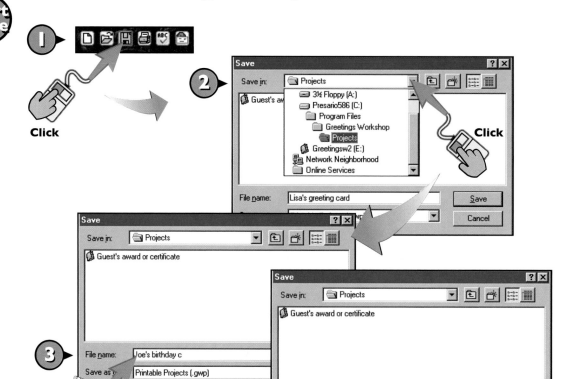

Start Here

Click

✓ Saving Changes to a Project

After you save and name your project file, click the **Save Project** button and then click **Save** to save your recent changes. You should resave the project every 10 minutes or so.

1 ► Click the **Save Project** button.

2 ► If needed, click the **Save In** list to choose another disk and folder in which to save the file.

3 ► Edit the **File Name** text box entry as needed.

4 ► Click the **Save** button.

Task 10: Opening an Existing Project

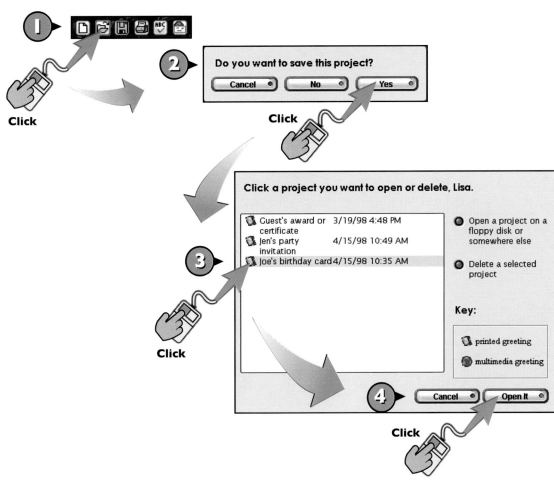

Click

Do you want to save this project?

Cancel   No   Yes

Click

Click

Click a project you want to open or delete, Lisa.

Guest's award or   3/19/98 4:48 PM
certificate
Jen's party   4/15/98 10:49 AM
invitation
Joe's birthday card 4/15/98 10:35 AM

○ Open a project on a
floppy disk or
somewhere else

○ Delete a selected
project

Key:

printed greeting

multimedia greeting

Cancel   Open It

Click

Reopening a Project

Any time you're using
Greetings Workshop, you
can stop what you're doing
and open a project you
worked with earlier. After
you open the project, you
can make changes to it,
save it, and print it.

✓ Opening from the Opening Screen
If you just started Greetings
Workshop and you're at the
opening screen where you
choose a new project to
create, you can click the
Open an Existing Project
choice that Rocky presents
to open an existing project
file.

✓ Finding Stored Projects
If the project you want to
open doesn't appear in the
list of projects (step 3),
click the **Open a Project
on a Floppy Disk or
Somewhere Else** button,
use the **Save In** list to
choose the disk and folder
holding the project to
open, click the project
name, and click **Open**.

1▸ Click the **Open Project** button.

2▸ If prompted, make sure you click **Yes** to save your changes to the current project.
Greetings Workshop closes that project.

3▸ Click the name of the project to open.

4▸ Click the **Open It** button.

Task 11: Printing and Exiting

Finishing Your Work

Printing your project enables you to give copies to other people, or in the case of posters and banners, display it with pride. After you print your project, if you've finished working, you can exit Greetings Workshop.

✓ Following Rocky's Advice

Rather than click a button at the top of the screen, you can click one of the choices that Rocky offers. (The choices change depending on what you're currently doing.) For example, Rocky often offers the **Print My Project** choice.

⚠ WARNING

The correct orientation—Portrait (tall) or Landscape (wide)—varies depending on the project type. You can't change this choice in the Print Setup dialog box unless you choose another printer.

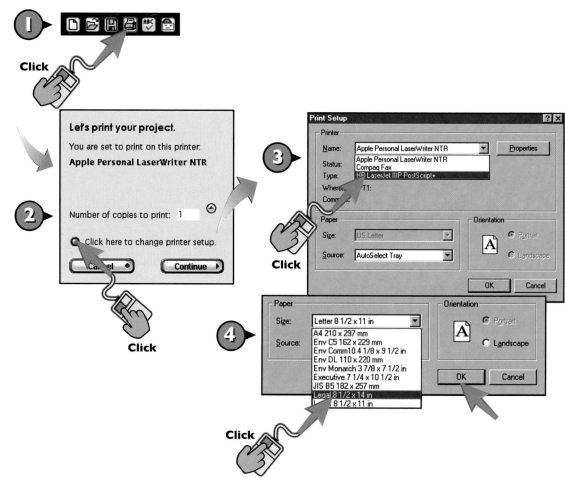

---

1 ▶ Click the **Print Project** button.

2 ▶ If your computer has more than one printer connected to it, click the **Click Here to Change Printer Setup** button.

3 ▶ Select the printer to use from the **Name** drop-down list.

4 ▶ If you want to use a paper size that's different from the default specified by the project, choose it from the **Size** drop-down list. Click the **OK** button.

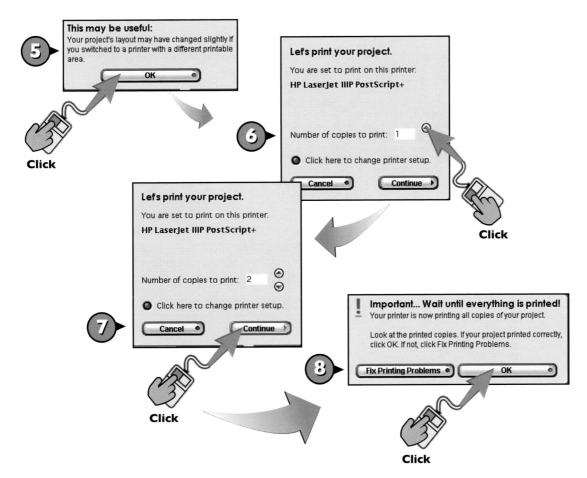

This may be useful:
Your project's layout may have changed slightly if you switched to a printer with a different printable area.

OK

Click

Let's print your project.

You are set to print on this printer:

HP LaserJet IIIP PostScript+

Number of copies to print: 1

Click here to change printer setup.

Cancel   Continue ▸

Click

Let's print your project.

You are set to print on this printer:

HP LaserJet IIIP PostScript+

Number of copies to print: 2

Click here to change printer setup.

Cancel   Continue ▸

Click

! Important... Wait until everything is printed!
Your printer is now printing all copies of your project.

Look at the printed copies. If your project printed correctly, click OK. If not, click Fix Printing Problems.

Fix Printing Problems   OK

Click

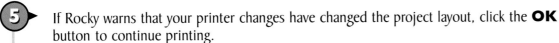

5 If Rocky warns that your printer changes have changed the project layout, click the **OK** button to continue printing.

6 Click the **Number of Copies to Print** up arrow button to increase the number of copies to print.

7 Click the **Continue** button. Rocky informs you that the project is printing.

8 Inspect your printout and click **OK**. Click the **Exit** at the bottom of the screen, then click **Yes**, if needed, to save the project before closing.

✓ **Emailing a Project**
Rather than printing a project, you can email it to other users, who can then view the project using Web browser software. Or you can save it to a floppy disk and mail it the old-fashioned way. To start the process for sending a project, click the **Send** button. Rocky then helps you decide on the best way to send your project and leads you through the rest of the steps.

✓ **Minimizing and Maximizing**
To minimize the Greetings Workshop application window to a taskbar icon, click the **Minimize** choice at the bottom of the Greetings Workshop screen. Then click its button on the taskbar to redisplay Greetings Workshop.

End Task

Task 12: Starting Encarta

Launching the Encarta Encyclopedia

While you can search the Web for information about nearly any topic, don't view the Microsoft Encarta 98 Encyclopedia as a "stepchild" with inferior information. In fact, you can benefit in a few ways by using Encarta. First, Encarta may be faster, depending on the topic you're searching for and the speed of your connection. Second, if your kids use Encarta, they won't be running across adult material on the Web. And Encarta requires neither a phone line nor an Internet account, so there's no additional expense in using it.

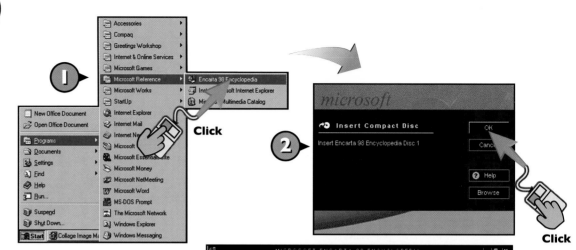

Click

Click

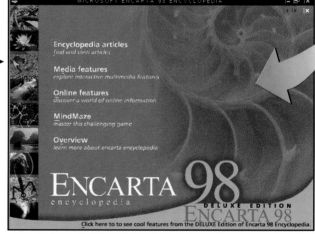

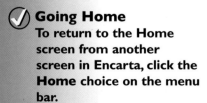

✓ Going Home
To return to the Home screen from another screen in Encarta, click the **Home** choice on the menu bar.

 Click **Start**, then **Programs**, point to **Microsoft Reference**, and then click **Encarta 98 Encyclopedia**.

 When prompted, insert the first Encarta CD-ROM (Disc 3 in Home Essentials) into your CD-ROM drive and click **OK**.

3 Start working in Encarta.

Task 13: Accessing Encarta Help

Start Here

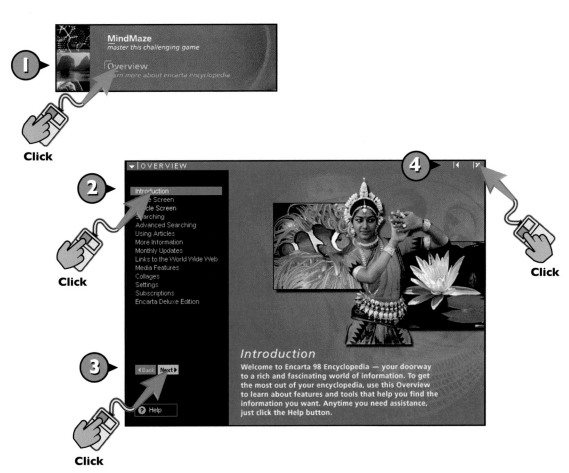

Click

Click

Click

Click

Getting Help in Encarta

Right off the bat, you can see that Encarta looks a little different than other Windows applications you've seen so far in this book. From the opening Encarta screen (called the Home screen), you can access a Help overview screen that tells you more about Encarta and how to use it to find information.

✓ **Displaying a Help Window**
After you begin reading Encarta articles, you can open the ? menu and click Help to display a Help topics window. This window works like those found in other Windows applications, as described in Part 6, Task 5, "Getting Help in an Application." You also can display a Help window by clicking the Help button in the lower-left corner of the Overview help screen.

Click the **Overview** choice.

To read help about a particular topic, click it in the list at the left.

To read the next page about a topic, click the **Next** button.

Click the **Close** button in the upper-right corner of the Overview window to return to the Encarta Home screen.

End Task

Task 14: Finding an Article by Title

Searching for a Topic

Encarta organizes information alphabetically in articles. Each article title corresponds to an alphabetical entry in an encyclopedia volume. But instead of flipping through the pages of a bound volume to find the topic you want, in Encarta you type the article name.

✓ Using the Pinpointer

The Pinpointer dialog box enables you to specify the article title or other item to search for. Task 15 explains how to move it out of the way.

ⓘ WARNING

After you use the technique of your choice to find articles and list them in the Pinpointer, click the **New Search** button to start again. Otherwise, your previous search technique remains active, and then the new search narrows the previous list of articles. So, you may not see all the applicable articles.

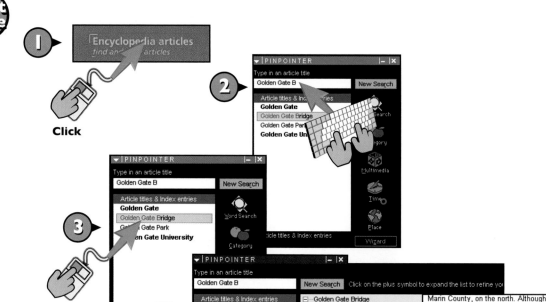

 Click the **Encyclopedia Articles** choice in the Home screen to display the Article screen.

 Type the article title (or even part of it) to find in the text box at the top of the Pinpointer.

To view an article, click it in the **Article Titles & Index Entries** list.

 If the Pinpointer expands to display additional choices, click the one you want. (Click the scroll bar to read more of the article.)

Task 15: Redisplaying and Closing the Pinpointer

Start Here

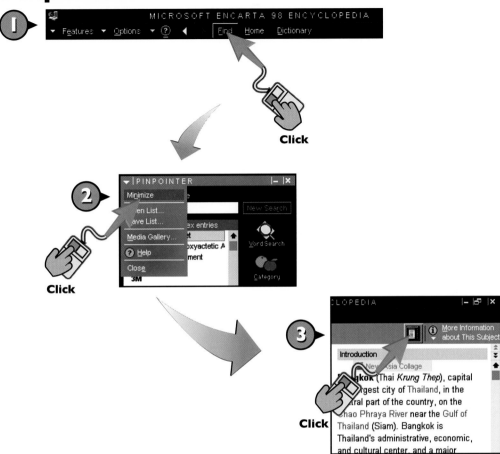

Click

Click

Click

Viewing and Hiding the Pinpointer

When you select an article that you want to read, Encarta automatically puts away the Pinpointer so that the maximum amount of information can appear on-screen. When you're ready to search for another article, you redisplay the Pinpointer to do so, or you can back up from the Pinpointer and redisplay the previous article.

⚠ WARNING

You can close the Pinpointer altogether or minimize it to an icon above the article. If you close the Pinpointer by clicking its window **Close** button or by choosing **Close** from its **Control** menu, you can only click **Find** to redisplay it. Closing the Pinpointer also clears the search settings in it, so you don't have to click **New Search** after you click **Find**.

1 ▶ With the Pinpointer closed, click **Find** on the Article screen menu bar to redisplay the Pinpointer.

2 ▶ To minimize (hide) the Pinpointer, click **Minimize** in its Control menu.

3 ▶ Click the Pinpointer's icon in the bar above the article to redisplay it.

End Task

Finding Articles That Hold a Certain Word

You can use the Pinpointer to search for information in a variety of ways. You aren't limited to typing in a topic. The next four tasks in the book cover alternate ways to use the Pinpointer. This task starts by explaining how to search for information based on one word, two words, or a phrase you enter.

✓ **Reviewing the Results**
These alternate search techniques also enable you to find multiple articles and then to select the one that provides the information you need.

✓ **Displaying the Article Screen**
If you're at the Home screen, don't forget to click the Encyclopedia Articles choice to redisplay the Article screen.

Task 16: Searching for a Word

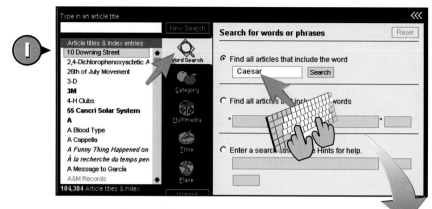

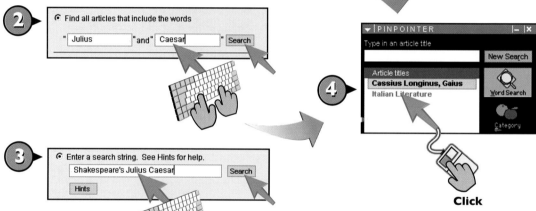

Click

① Click the **Word Search** button and a word to search for in the text box under **Find All Articles that Include the Word**.

② To search for two words, click **Find All Articles that Include the Words**, then enter the words in the accompanying text boxes.

③ To search for a phrase, click **Enter a Search String**, then type the phrase in the accompanying text box.

④ Click the **Search** button beside your choice, then click the title of the article to read.

Task 17: Finding an Article by Category

Start Here

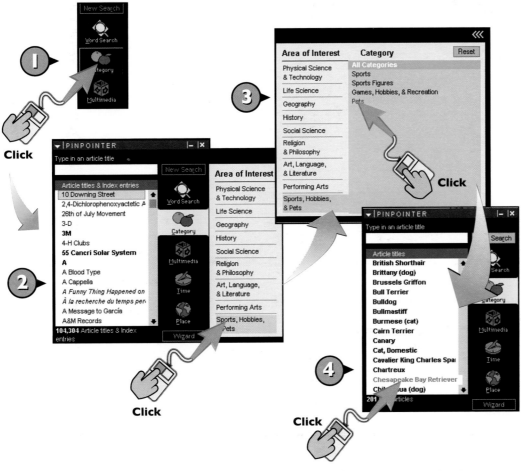

Click

Click

Click

Click

Specifying a Category to Find Articles

In addition to organizing articles alphabetically, Encarta groups them by area of interest and category. So if you're interested in finding out more about something and want to see a list of articles about that subject area, try searching by category.

1. Click the **Category** button in the Pinpointer.

2. Click an **Area of Interest** to list the categories it holds.

3. Click the category that holds the articles you want in the **Category** list.

4. Click the article you want to read in the **Article Titles** list.

✅ **Resetting the Search**
Once you've displayed a list of categories in the Pinpointer, click the Reset button to choose another area of interest and its list of categories.

End Task

Task 18: Finding an Article by Time

Searching by Date

History students want to know *when* things happened, not just who did what and why. Encarta can help you find out more about events that happened and people who lived at about the same time.

✓ How Date Searches Can Help

Searching for articles by time is a good way to select a subject for a school report. For example, say you know the Renaissance occurred around the year 1500. You can search for that date and scan through the listed articles for different Renaissance artists and scientists.

! WARNING

Don't forget to click **New Search** in the Pinpointer after you perform any type of search. If two of the search type buttons in the Pinpointer are highlighted, that means you have more than one set of search settings active, so you may need to click **New Search**.

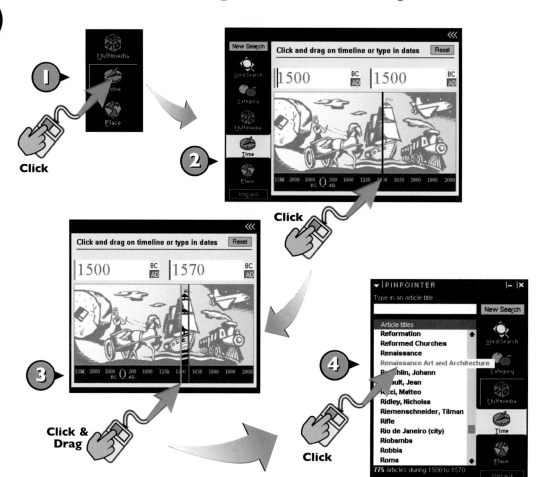

Click

Click

Click & Drag

Click

> **1** Click the **Time** button in the Pinpointer.

> **2** To specify a single year, click it in the timeline or type it in the first text box.

> **3** To specify a period of years, drag in the timeline or enter the starting and ending dates in the text boxes.

> **4** Click the article you want to read in the **Article Titles** list.

Task 19: Finding an Article by Place

Start Here

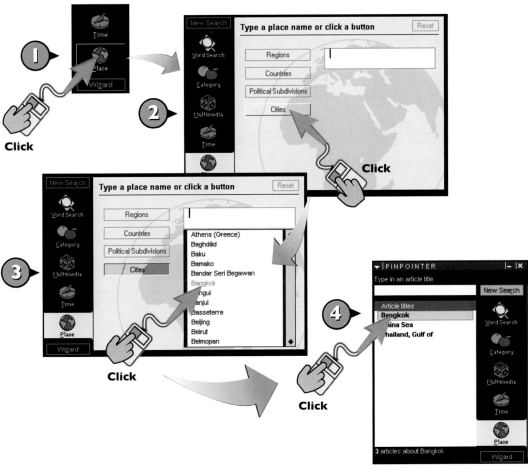

Click

Click

Click

Click

Searching for Information About a Place

If you want to find out more about a region of the world, country, or city, you can find all the Encarta articles relating to it.

1 ▶ Click the **Place** button in the Pinpointer.

2 ▶ Click the type of place you want to search for.

3 ▶ In the list that appears, click the specific place about which you want to see articles.

4 ▶ Click the article you want to read in the **Article Titles** list.

✓ **Understanding Political Subdivisions**
In Encarta, a *political subdivision* is a state, province, or other smaller entity within a country.

End Task

Task 20: Discovering What the Media Icons Mean

Start Here

Reviewing Article Icons

If you've looked at any articles, you may have seen small icons listed at the top of the article or in the Outline list to the left of the Article screen. Each of these icons represents some type of media object or media clip with more information about the article. There are a number of different media types, so this Task presents a shortcut method of finding out what each icon means and finding articles that include a particular type of media.

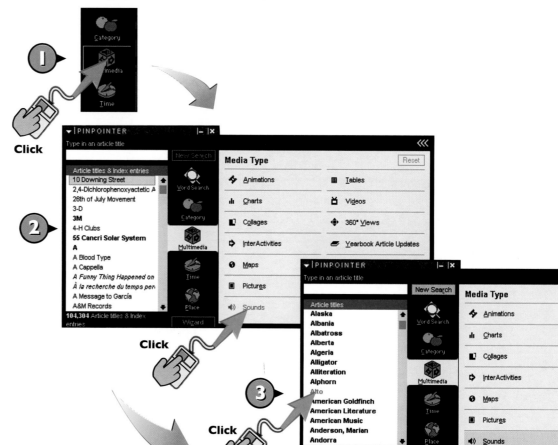

Click

Click

Click

✓ **Finding More about Media**
Tasks 22 and 23 explain how to work with a couple of types of media.

1 ▶ Click the **Multimedia** button in the Pinpointer.

2 ▶ Review the different types of media and the icons representing them in the expanded Pinpointer. To list articles using a particular media type, click that media type in the list.

3 ▶ Click the article you want to read in the **Article Titles** list.

End Task

Task 21: Viewing a Topic Within an Article

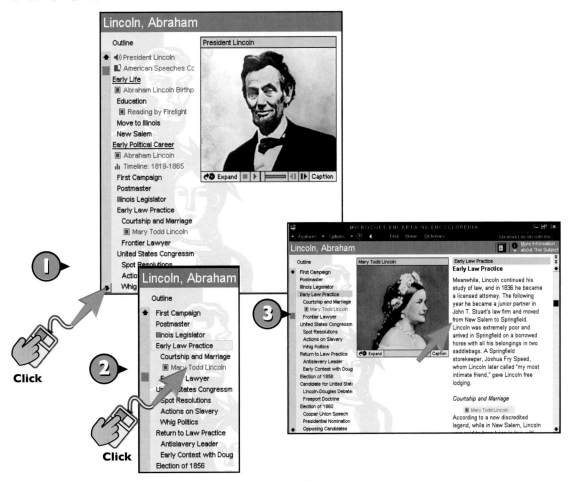

Lincoln, Abraham

Outline

◆ ◀)) President Lincoln
◻ 📖 American Speeches Co

Early Life
◻ Abraham Lincoln Birthp
Education
◻ Reading by Firelight
Move to Illinois
New Salem
Early Political Career
◻ Abraham Lincoln
📊 Timeline: 1819-1865
First Campaign
Postmaster
Illinois Legislator
Early Law Practice
   Courtship and Marriage
   ◻ Mary Todd Lincoln
Frontier Lawyer
United States Congressm
   Spot Resolutions
   Actio
Whig

President Lincoln

⟲ Expand ◼ ▶ ◀◀ ▶▶ Caption

Lincoln, Abraham

Outline

◆ First Campaign
Postmaster
Illinois Legislator
Early Law Practice
   Courtship and Marriage
   ◻ Mary Todd Lincoln
   F... Lawyer
Un...states Congressm
   Spot Resolutions
   Actions on Slavery
   Whig Politics
Return to Law Practice
   Antislavery Leader
   Early Contest with Doug
Election of 1856

MICROSOFT ENCARTA 98 ENCYCLOPEDIA

Features ▾ Options ▾ ⑦ ◀ Find Home Dictionary Abraham Lincoln with link:

Lincoln, Abraham

Outline

◆ First Campaign
Postmaster
Illinois Legislator
Early Law Practice
   Courtship and Marriage
   ◻ Mary Todd Lincoln
   Frontier Lawyer
United States Congressm
   Spot Resolutions
   Actions on Slavery
   Whig Politics
Return to Law Practice
   Antislavery Leader
   Early Contest with Doug
Election of 1856
Candidate for United Stat
Lincoln-Douglas Debate:
   Freeport Doctrine
Election of 1860
   Cooper Union Speech
   Presidential Nomination
   Opposing Candidates

Mary Todd Lincoln

⟲ Expand Caption

More Information about This Subject

Early Law Practice

Meanwhile, Lincoln continued his study of law, and in 1836 he became a licensed attorney. The following year he became a junior partner in John T. Stuart's law firm and moved from New Salem to Springfield. Lincoln was extremely poor and arrived in Springfield on a borrowed horse with all his belongings in two saddlebags. A Springfield storekeeper, Joshua Fry Speed, whom Lincoln later called "my most intimate friend," gave Lincoln free lodging.

Courtship and Marriage

◻ Mary Todd Lincoln

According to a now discredited legend, while in New Salem, Lincoln...

① Click

②

③

Click

Reading an Article Topic

Just as you would divide up a lengthy report by adding headings and subheadings, Encarta divides its longer articles into more manageable topics. The outline at the left side of the Article screen lists the topics and subtopics within the current article. You can use that outline to navigate to different topics within the article.

  Use the scroll bar at the left of the Outline to scroll through the topics.

  Click a topic in the list to display it.

  Review the specified topic at the left side of the screen.

 Backing Up in an Article
You can use the left arrow button on the Article screen menu bar to back up to the previous topic or screen of information.

Task 22: Viewing a Graphic

Opening an Article Graphic

To save space onscreen so you can read more of an article, Encarta crops most of the pictures (graphic images) contained in articles. You can view a caption for the picture, or you can expand a picture to see more of it and see the caption included for it, and then return it to its original size when you finish.

✓ **Inserting the CD-ROM**
When you try to expand some pictures (or work with other types of media in an article), Encarta may prompt you to insert the second Encarta CD. Insert the **Home Essentials Disc 4 CD-ROM** into your CD-ROM drive, then click **OK**.

✓ **Printing a Graphic**
After you expand a picture, you can open the **Control** menu for its window, then click **Print Image** or **Print Caption** to print the picture or caption.

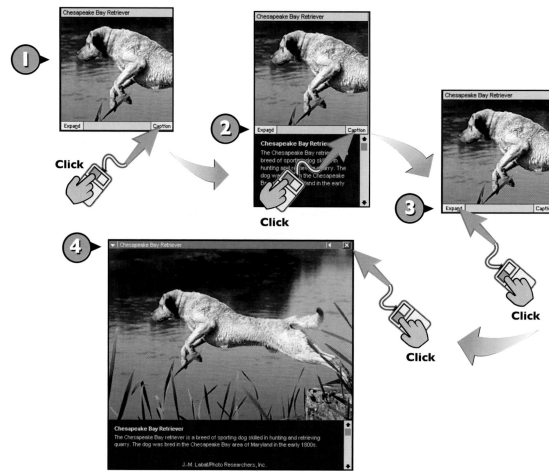

Click the **Caption** button at the bottom of the picture.

After you read the caption, click the **Caption** button again to close it.

Click the **Expand** button to enlarge the picture and display its caption.

Click the **Close** button to return it to its original size.

Task 23: Listening to an Audio Clip

Start Here

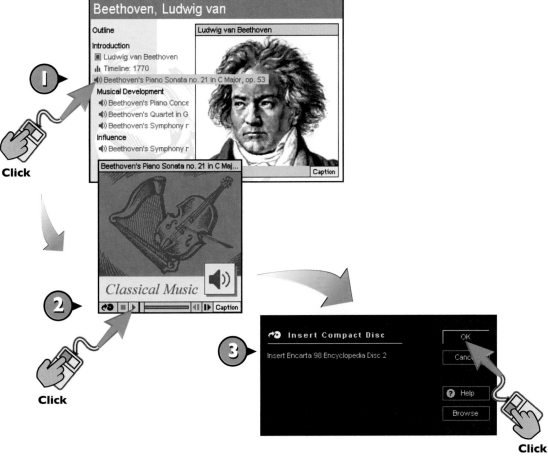

Click

Click

Click

Playing a Sound from an Article

To make your learning experiences more enjoyable and memorable, some Encarta articles include sounds (audio clips) that you can play. After all, what's more clear, a description of a composer's music or a sample of it? A description of a speech or a spoken excerpt from it? A description of an animal's call or the call itself? Be on the lookout for sound icons in your articles and play them when you want to hear about as well as read about a topic.

1. Click the **Sound** icon for the sound you want to play in the article text or outline.

2. Click the **Play** button at the bottom of the window for the clip.

3. Insert the Home Essentials Disc 4 CD-ROM into your CD-ROM drive and click **OK** to play the sound.

End Task

Task 24: Printing an Article

Making a Hard Copy

If you have more than one person clamoring to look up information in Encarta or want to read your information in a comfortable setting away from your computer, you can print it. In fact, you can print all or part of the article.

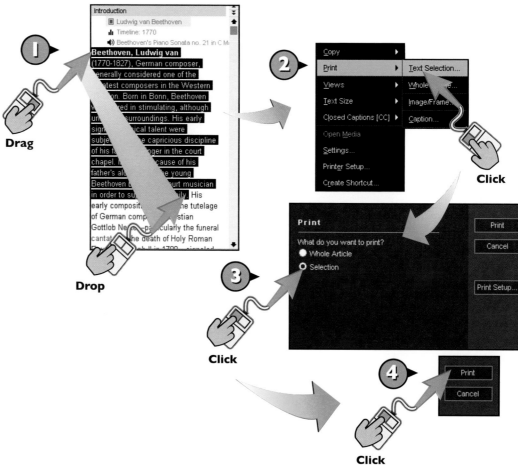

1. Drag to select text to print in an article, if desired.

2. Choose **Options**, **Print**, **Text Selection**.

3. Click an option button to choose whether you want to print the **Whole Article** or the **Selection**.

4. Click the **Print** button to print.

Task 25: Exiting Encarta

Start Here

Click

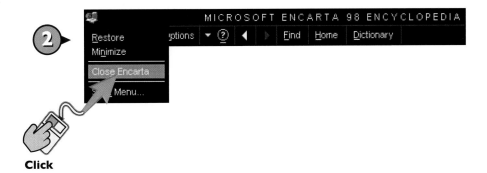
Click

Closing Encarta

When you finish working with Encarta, you should exit the program to remove it from your computer's memory. Because Encarta relies on **CD-ROM** data, you also need to exit Encarta if you want to run another application that uses a **CD-ROM** or if you want to play an audio **CD** while you work.

1 Open the **Control** menu for the Encarta application window.

2 Click **Close Encarta**.

End Task

PART 6

Refreshing Your Windows Skills

When version 3.1 of Windows arrived, software publishers began to incorporate aspects of its look and feel into applications. Over time, Windows applications (applications that run under Windows) have adapted to become more and more standard. This helps you navigate as easily in one program as you would in any other. This part reminds you how to perform basic tasks common to Windows applications. The tasks show you applications displayed from Windows 95. If you're using the newer Windows 98 system, your screens will look slightly different, but most of the steps described here will be the same.

Tasks

Reviewing an Application Window

When you start a Windows program, it opens in its own window called the *application window*. While you work with file information within the application window, you can perform certain tasks and get information using the parts of the application window itself.

Different Windows, Same Features

In most applications, each document (file) also opens in its own window. A file window has some of the same features as an application window. The parts of a file window work just like the corresponding parts of an application window.

Task 1: Reviewing Parts of an Application Window

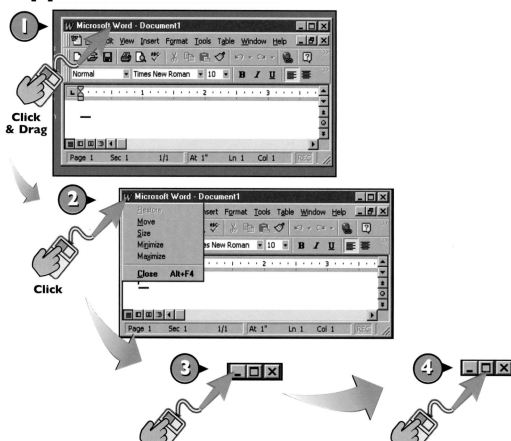

Click & Drag

Click

Click

Click

When the window isn't full-sized (maximized), you can drag the title bar, which displays the application name.

Click the **Control Menu box** to display the Control menu, which offers commands for sizing and moving the window.

Click the **Minimize** button (right end of the title bar) to reduce the application to a Windows taskbar button. Click that button to redisplay the application.

Click the **Maximize** button (right end of the title bar) to increase the window to full-screen size. To downsize the window again, click the **Restore** button that appears.

Next Step

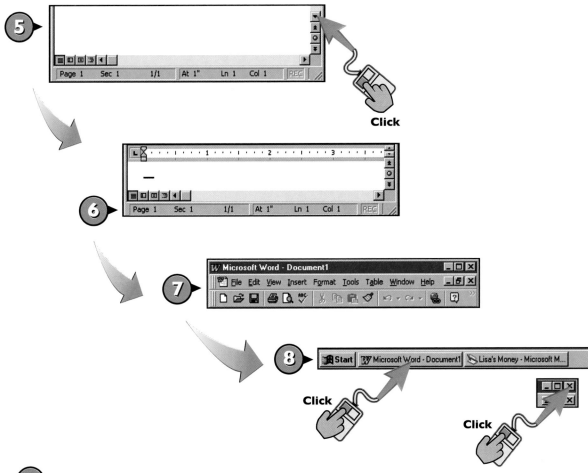

Click

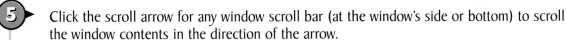

Click   **Click**

Resizing with the Title Bar
You also can resize a window via the title bar. If the window isn't maximized (full size), double-click the title bar to maximize it. Double-click the title bar again to restore it to its previous size.

Dragging to Resize a Window
When the window isn't maximized (full-sized), drag its border to resize it.

Dragging to Scroll
You also can drag the scroll box on the scrollbar to scroll more quickly.

5 ▶ Click the scroll arrow for any window scroll bar (at the window's side or bottom) to scroll the window contents in the direction of the arrow.

6 ▶ Check the status bar at the bottom of the application window for information about the application and currently opened file.

7 ▶ Choose commands using the menu bar or toolbar.

8 ▶ Click an application button on the Windows taskbar to switch to that application. Click the **Close** button (right end of the title bar) to exit the application.

End Task

Selecting a Menu Command

You select a command to tell an application what action to perform. Windows applications hold commands on menus. After you open a menu, its commands appear. If a triangle appears to the right of a command, moving the mouse pointer over that command displays a submenu with more command choices. If a check mark appears to the left of a command, selecting that command toggles it off (unchecking it) or on (checking it). If an ellipsis (...) appears to the right of a command, selecting the command displays a dialog box so you can specify more details, as described in Task 4.

✅ **Other Ways to Choose Commands**
You can click a toolbar button to perform some commands. To find the right button, point to the toolbar until a description for the button appears.

Task 2: Selecting a Command from a Menu

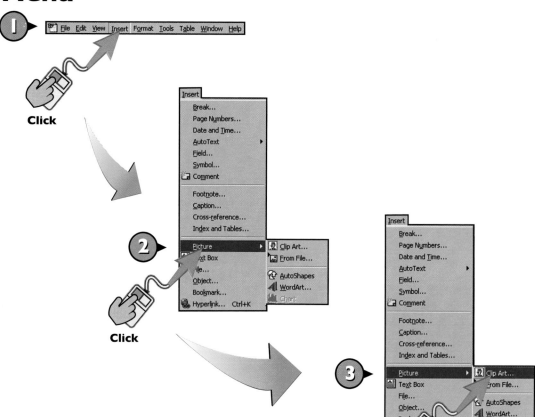

Click

Click

Click

 Click the menu name in the title bar.

 Move the mouse pointer down the menu to highlight the command you want.

 If a submenu appears, drag the mouse to point to a command in the submenu. Click the command to select it.

End Task

Task 3: Selecting a Command from a Shortcut Menu

Start Here

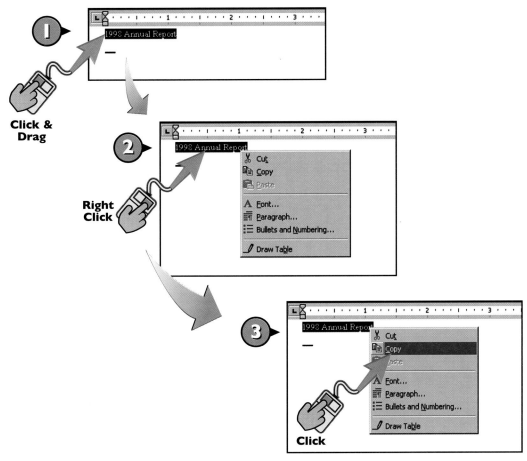

Click & Drag

Right Click

Click

Using Shortcut Menus

Shortcut menus provide a faster means of identifying the commands you need. Rather than searching through all the menus or toolbar buttons, you can simply right-click to display a more succinct menu of commands. Shortcut menus are also called *context menus* in some applications because they present command options related to (in the context of) what you're already doing.

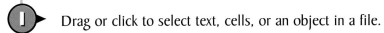

1 Drag or click to select text, cells, or an object in a file.

2 Right-click the selection.

3 Move the mouse pointer down the menu to highlight the command you want. Click the command to select it.

✓ Decoding Commands

As for commands listed on a menu bar menu, a command on a shortcut menu may be followed by an ellipsis or triangle, meaning that that command displays a dialog box or submenu after you select it.

End Task

Task 4: Responding to a Dialog Box

Dealing with a Dialog Box

Choosing a command with an ellipsis beside it opens a dialog box so that you can specify more detail about how the application should perform a command. Dialog boxes can be very simple, or they might display dozens of choices. Dialog boxes contain different types of controls, such as check boxes and command buttons, that you use to make your choices. This task reviews these controls and how to use them.

✓ Clicking to Specify a Value

A text box may include up and down arrows at its right end; these are called spinner buttons. Click the **up arrow** button to increase the value in the text box and the **down arrow** button to decrease it.

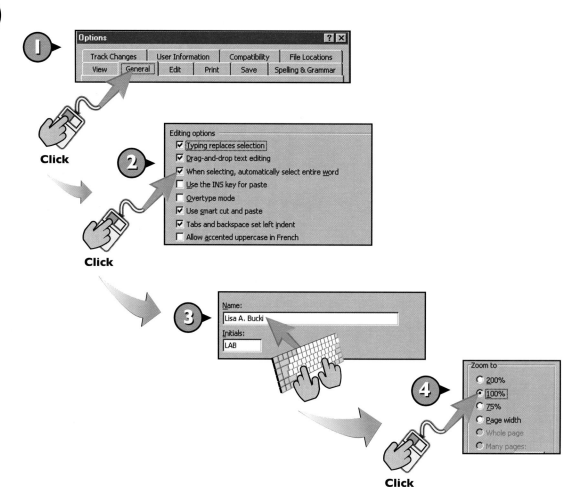

Click

Click

Click

1 Click a tab to display the options it holds.

2 Click a check box to check (select) it or clear (deselect) it.

3 Click in a text box and type to make an entry.

4 Click an option button to select it and deselect the other options in the group.

Next Step

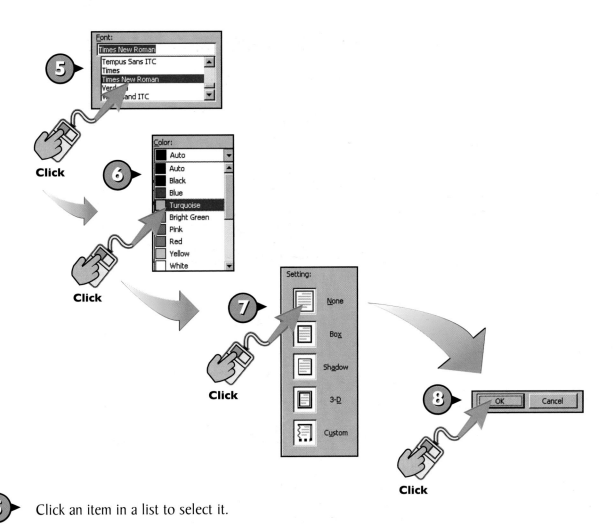

5 Click an item in a list to select it.

6 Click the drop-down list arrow to open a drop-down list and click a choice in the list.

7 If the dialog box offers buttons, icons, or pictures, select your choice.

8 Click a command button to display another dialog box or perform a command. Clicking the **OK** button accepts your choices and closes the dialog box.

⚠ WARNING
Don't press Enter before you've specified all your choices in a dialog box. Generally, pressing **Enter** accepts your choices, closes the dialog box, and executes the commands using the options you specified—even if they were incomplete.

✓ Canceling a Dialog Box
You can click the **Cancel** button to close a dialog box without completing the command or applying its options.

Task 5: Getting Help in an Application

Getting Help

Software programs include an online Help system that you can consult to find out the steps for a task. The Help system also offers definitions, overview information, and other types of coverage to ensure that you understand what to do. The Help system in some applications also provides you with multimedia application tours and information about contacting technical support or finding online resources specific to the application.

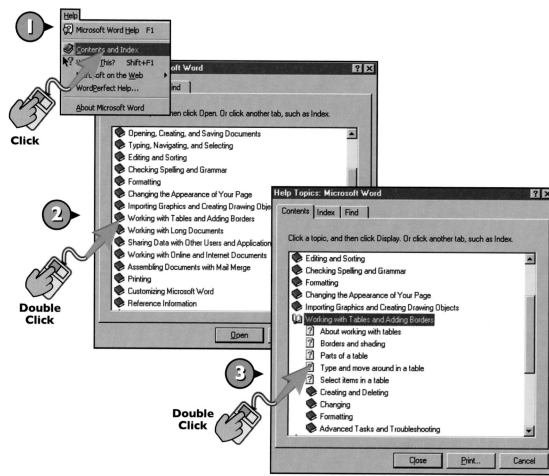

1. Choose **Help**, **Help Contents** (or the Help command for your application).

2. Double-click a book icon to open it and display a list of topics.

3. Double-click a page icon to see help about that topic.

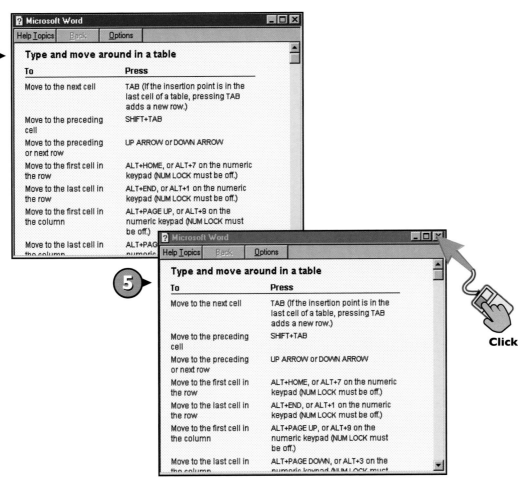

Click

Review the information in the Help window that appears.

You can click the **Help Topics** button and repeat steps I through 6 to view additional help. Or click the Help window's **Close** button to exit Help.

 Opening Other Book Icons

When you double-click some book icons in the Help Topics window, the list that appears includes other book icons. Double-click one of those icons, as well, to open it.

Setting Up Your Internet Connection

Internet Explorer 3.02 (part of Home Essentials 98) includes the **Internet Connection Wizard (ICW)**. You use the ICW to set up a Dial-Up Networking connection under Windows so that your modem can dial in to your Internet account (via a phone line in your home) to connect with the Internet. The ICW walks you through the connection setup process, step by step.

You sign up for an Internet account with an **Internet service provider (ISP)**. ISPs generally charge a flat monthly fee for Internet access. If you already have an Internet account, you do need to run the ICW to set up your system to dial the account. If you don't have an Internet account, you can use the ICW to connect to the Internet Referral Service's list of national ISPs with which you can obtain an account.

 PPP Connection
When you get an account with an ISP, be sure to ask for a PPP (Point-to-Point Protocol) connection. Make sure the access phone number you get for dialing in to your account is a local call. If you travel much, you'll want a provider that has a toll-free access number, too.

The **Dial-Up Networking** connection (also called simply your Internet connection) that the ICW creates uses **TCP/IP** for connecting to the Internet. What you need to know about TCP/IP is that it connects you to your ISP in such a way that you can run Windows-based graphical software such as Internet Explorer 3.02 to work with the Internet by pointing and clicking.

 WARNING
Some ISPs provide software to set up the Internet Connection for you so that you don't have to gather the information listed next. If you sign up with the Microsoft Network (MSN), for example, you'll use a different setup process. You only need to use the ICW if your ISP doesn't provide setup software or if you opt not to use the ISP's software. On the other hand, if there are glitches in the ISP's setup software and it doesn't quite work for you, try the ICW instead.

Before you run the ICW to set up the connection, gather these pieces of information from your Internet Service Provider:

- *ISP phone number.* This is the number you dial to connect.

- *User name and password.* Your ISP provides these when you create your account.

- *IP (Internet Protocol) addresses.* These are special numbers used to identify your ISP's servers on the Internet. IP addresses always have four sets of 1–3 numbers each, separated by periods. For example, 207.79.160.1 is an IP address. You need to know whether your ISP automatically (dynamically) assigns an ISP to your system when you log in. You also need to know the IP address for your ISP's Domain Name Service (DNS) server.

- *Login method.* If your ISP offers the PAP or CHAP protocols for logging in (you don't really need to know what these acronyms mean), you can set up your connection so it remembers your user name and password and provides them automatically when you connect.

Follow these steps to use the ICW to establish your Internet connection:

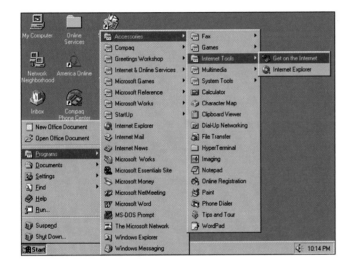

I   Click **Start**, point to **Programs**, and then to **Accessories**. On the Accessories menu, point to **Internet Tools** and click **Get on the Internet** (or **Internet Setup Wizard**). Alternatively, you can double-click the **Internet** icon on the desktop if you haven't previously used the Internet Connection Wizard; if you have, this

icon launches Internet Explorer instead. (If you upgraded to Windows 98, the Setup program probably prompted you to set up your Internet connection. If not, choose **Start**, point to **Programs**, then to **Internet Explorer**, and click **Connection Wizard**. This starts the Windows 98 ICW. Follow its onscreen steps, which are similar to those listed here.)

2   The first Internet Connection Wizard (ICW) dialog box appears. Click **Next**. In the next ICW dialog box, select how to set up your computer.

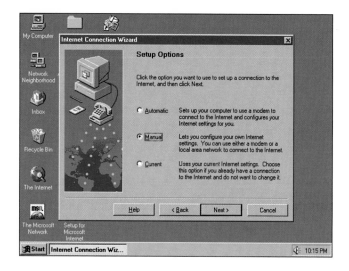

3 If you don't already have an account with an ISP, click **Automatic** and follow the rest of the wizard, which installs connection software and then logs you on to the Internet Referral Service, which you can use to sign up with an ISP. (After you sign up, the ICW should restart automatically. If it doesn't, restart these steps to use the ICW to set up your new connection, after the ISP provides the logon information you need.) If you already have an account, click **Manual**, then click **Next**. The rest of these steps assume you have an account with an ISP and clicked Manual.

4 In the ICW Welcome dialog box, click **Next**.

5 Assuming you're a home user and will be connecting to the Internet with a modem, leave **Connect Using My Phone Line** selected in the next ICW dialog box, and then click **Next**.

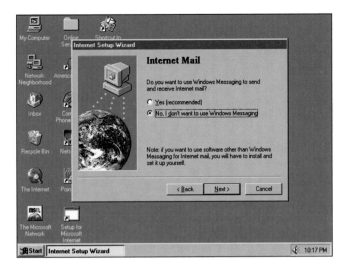

6 In the next ICW dialog box, click **No, I Don't Want to Use Windows Messaging**. You do this because you probably want to use another, more user-friendly Internet email program. (Windows 95 OSR2 offers the Internet Mail email program, while Windows 98 offers Outlook Express; if you haven't been using an Internet email program, either of these programs will work well for home Internet email.) Click **Next**.

WARNING

After step 6, the Internet Connection Wizard may prompt you to select your modem. If it does, choose your modem and click Next to continue with the Internet Connection Wizard.

7 If ICW tells you it's going to begin installing files, which it doesn't do in every case, click **Next**. If Windows prompts you to insert your installation CD or disks, do so.

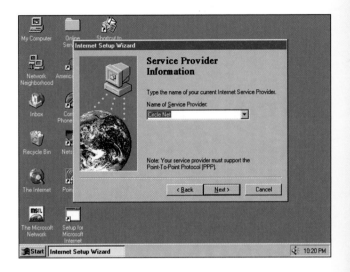

8 ICW begins prompting you for information about your ISP. The first screen asks you for the **Name of Service Provider**. Enter it, and then click **Next**.

9 In the next ICW dialog box, enter the phone number for your ISP, including area code. Leave the other settings as is. Click **Next**.

10 Enter your **User Name** and **Password**. Click **Next**.

11 Most users can usually click **Next** at this ICW dialog box because most ISPs dynamically assign an IP address each time you connect.

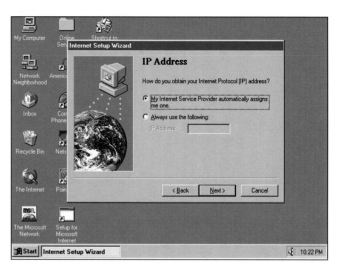

12 Enter the **DNS Server** IP addresses for your ISP. Click **Next**.

13 At the ICW dialog box that tells you the
connection is complete, click **Finish**.

14 At the dialog box that prompts you to restart
your computer, click **Yes**. The computer restarts
and updates your system's settings.

account   A Money 98 account represents each savings, checking, or investment account you have in the real world. You use each Money account you create to hold the transactions for that account and to calculate the current account balance.

alignment   How text lines up relative to the document margin or cell border. Text can align to the left or right, or can be centered between the margins or borders.

application window   Holds the application menus, buttons, the file or data you're working with, and other features.

automatic page break   See *soft page break*

browser   *See Web browser*

browsing   Moving from Web page to Web page using browser software.

button   An onscreen icon (picture button) or area you click to perform a command or follow a link. Many of the Home Essentials applications offer a toolbar filled with buttons near the top of the application window.

category   A label used in Money 98 to identify an income or expense so that Money can report how you spend your money and where it comes from.

checking account   A Money 98 account that corresponds to your real-world checking account. You can enter bills in the checking account and use Money to print checks to pay those bills.

clip art   Pre-drawn artwork you can insert in a document in Word 97 or Works 4.5.

Clipboard   A holding area in memory where your computer stores information you've cut or copied from a document.

command   A menu choice that directs the application to perform a particular action, such as saving or printing a file.

concepts   Groupings of categories and subcategories that provide still further reporting effectiveness in Money.

content identifier   The initial portion of an Internet address (URL), which identifies what kind of information the address holds. The content identifier for Web addresses is **http/**.

context menu   *See shortcut menu*

cut   To remove the selected information from the file and place it in the Windows Clipboard. You can then paste this information to a new location in the document or even to another document or application.

database   A program that enables you to store and organize lists of data, such as an address book list or home inventory.

Dial-Up Networking   Windows' capability for connecting to and communicating with an online network via your modem. Windows enables you to create a Dial-Up Networking connection to dial into your Internet account.

document   A letter, memo, report, or other text-based file created in a word processing program.

document window (file window)   The window that holds an individual file within an application window.

download   To transfer a file from the Internet or another computer to your computer via modem, so you can save it.

drag and drop   To move or copy a selection by dragging it with the mouse and dropping it into place.

field   In a database program, one piece of information that appears in every entry (called a record), such as the *last name* for address entries.

file   A single document, spreadsheet, or database, named and stored on disk.

Financial Organizer Software (Financial Management Software)   Software like Money 98, which tracks your bank and other investment accounts. These programs enable you to categorize income and expenses, print checks, and create budgets.

font   The particular design of the characters in a selection. Each font has a name, such as Arial or Times New Roman. You select the font by name to apply it to a selection.

formatting   Changes you make in the appearance of a selection or page. For example, you can make text bold or change the width of the margins (white space) around a page.

FTP (file transfer protocol)   The communication method that your Web browser uses to download (transfer) a file from an Internet location to your computer.

hard page break   A page break (new page start) that you insert where you want in a file, based on the file content and how you want it to look when printed.

highlighting   *See selecting*

home page   Also called the start page. The first page your browser displays when you connect to the Internet. (Also the main or initial page for a Web site.)

hyperlinks   *See links*

Insert mode   In Word 97 or the Works word processing tool, the mode where the word processor inserts text you type within existing text at the insertion point location. Existing text to the right of the insertion point moves right to accommodate the inserted text.

insertion point   The flashing vertical hash mark that indicates where typed text will appear in a document or dialog box.

Internet   The worldwide network of computers that stores and transfers information.

Internet account   Dial-up Internet access that you purchase from an Internet service provider. When you obtain an account, you receive an account name and password you use to connect and log on via your modem. Once you connect to your account (your Internet connection), you can use a browser to work on the Web, use your email, and so on.

Internet Connection Wizard (ICW)   A feature in Windows that leads you through the process of creating a Dial-Up Networking connection so your modem can dial up and connect to your Internet connection.

Internet service provider (ISP)   A company that sells Internet access. ISPs have large server computers with fast connections to the Internet. When you dial into your Internet account, your modem connects your computer to the ISP's server computer, which in turn connects your computer to the Internet.

links   Specially formatted text, buttons, or graphics you click on a Web page to display (jump to) a different Web page.

location   The second portion of an Internet address (URL), which identifies the server computer and directory storing the Web page that the address represents. **www.mcp.com/que/** is an example of how the location portion reads.

manual page break   See *hard page break*

maximize   To expand a window so it fills the screen (for an application window) or the available space within the application window (for a file or document window).

minimize   To reduce a window to a button on the taskbar (for an application window) or icon within the application window (for a file window).

modem   A device that enables your computer to communicate with another computer via telephone lines. (Newer types of modems enable your computer to communicate via special higher-speed phone lines, cable television connections, or even satellite.)

navigation bar   A bar below the menu bar in Money 98 that offers buttons for displaying different features and lists in Money, such as the Account Manager (list of accounts) and list of categories and payees.

Overtype mode In Word 97 or the Works word processing tool, the mode where the word processor types over (replaces) text to the right of the insertion point location.

paragraph break Pressing Enter to create a new paragraph in a word processing document.

paste Inserts information from the Windows Clipboard into a file, at the location you specify.

recognizing How a spell checker identifies misspelled words. It compares the words in your file with a dictionary, passing by words it recognizes and stopping on words it doesn't.

record In a database program, all the fields (individual pieces of information) for a single entry. For example, all the pieces of address information for one person would be a record.

recurring transaction In Money 98, a bill (check) or deposit

(such as a pay deposit) that happens at regular intervals. You set up Money 98 to remind you of a recurring transaction and enter the transaction information for you.

Redo After you undo a correction, in some applications you can redo it if you change your mind.

restore Using a backup copy of a file to replace the current version if it becomes damaged.

scroll Clicking a scroll bar to view a different area in a file or list.

search word A word or phrase you enter in a Web search tool to find Web pages covering the topic you entered.

selecting Using the mouse or keyboard to place highlighting over text (or display handles around an object) so that the next command you perform applies to the selection.

shareware Shareware is distributed via the honor system. If

you install and use shareware, you should mail the specified modest payment to its author.

shortcut menu A menu that appears when you right-click a selection, offering a concise list of commands you can perform on the selection.

soft page break A page break inserted automatically in an application when you enter enough information to fill the current page.

spreadsheet A file created in a spreadsheet program where you enter information in cells in a grid of rows and columns. You can then enter formulas (in other cells) to perform calculations.

Start menu The menu that appears when you click the Start button at the left end of the Windows taskbar. The Start menu enables you to access application startup commands, as well as startup commands for various Windows tools and applets.

start page   *See home page*

subcategory   A sublabel of a Money 98 category, used to identify an expense or income transaction more precisely. *See also category*

template   A file you can use to create a new document with predefined text and formatting. Most templates prompt you to fill in additional information and automatically format that information for you.

TCP/IP   The language or protocol that your Dial-Up Networking connection uses to communicate with your ISP server computer and other computers on the Internet.

toolbar button   *See button*

transaction   A bill (check), deposit, transfer, withdrawal, or cash machine action that you record in a Money 98 account.

Undo   Reverses a command or action.

Uniform Resource Locator (URL)   The address for a particular file on the Internet, such as the address for a particular Web page. Also called an Internet address or Web address.

virus   A hidden program or file that travels along with files you download or copy to your computer. A virus hides on your system until it's triggered by a particular date and time or action, and then the virus runs. A virus may be benign, doing no more than displaying a message on your screen. Or it may be malignant, destroying data or preventing your computer from working correctly. Use virus-checking software to identify and remove viruses.

Web (World Wide Web)   A subset of computers on the Internet that store information you can display graphically using a Web browser.

Web address   *See Uniform Resource Locator*

Web browser   A program that enables your computer to display graphic information downloaded via modem from the World Wide Web.

Windows   The operating system that runs your computer. Its name stems from its method of displaying applications and files within movable and resizable windows (borders) onscreen.

wizard   A helper program that leads you through a process and prompts you to enter information to complete the task.

word processing program   A program you use to create and print text-based documents.

word wrap   Applied primarily in word processing programs, word wrap occurs when text reaches the right margin or border (filling the current line) so that the insertion point automatically moves to the next line.

WordArt   In both Word and Works, used to apply a decorative effect, such as 3D or curving, to text you enter.

Symbols

displaying

E

Form view, Works databases